Drama
for
All
Occasions

Compiled by
John Lee Welton

Convention Press
Nashville, Tennessee

© Copyright 1991 • Convention Press
Reprinted 1998, 2000

ISBN 0-7673-1959-1

Dewey Decimal Classification: 792
Subject Heading: DRAMA

Printed in the United States of America

Church Recreation Program
Pastor-Staff Leadership Department
LifeWay Christian Resources
of the Southern Baptist Convention
127 Ninth Avenue, North
Nashville, TN 37234

CONTENTS

INTRODUCTION

ONE-ACT PLAYS

DRAMATIC AND COMEDY MESSAGE SKETCHES

MONOLOGUES

(For Males)

(For Females)

(For Both Males and Females)

READERS THEATRE AND CHORAL READING

FUN DRAMA FOR FELLOWSHIPS

Introduction

Drama for All Occasions includes scripts for church groups just beginning in the drama ministry, as well as groups who have an ongoing drama program and who are seeking plays of more breadth. For groups who are just beginning their drama ministry, it would perhaps be best to start with the shorter scripts in the "Dramatic and Comedy Message Sketches," or with the "Monologues," so that rehearsal schedule problems can be lessened.

A number of one-act plays have been included. Some of these reach beyond the typical "church play," but have a message that may speak more directly to current moral and ethical problems faced by Christians.

The section, "Readers Theatre and Choral Reading," is designed to provide group participation in short, effective dramatic offerings that are a slightly different approach from the standard play. A word of caution, however. To be effective, they should be as well rehearsed as any other dramatic presentation, perhaps even more so in the case of choral reading.

The final section is included to show that drama can be used just for fun as well as presenting a message. There are many occasions when good, Christian fellowship and fun can refresh the spirit with laughter.

Whatever form of drama ministry your group chooses, it is the prayer of all who have had a hand in writing and assembling this material that you may know the joy of sharing your God-given creative talents with others and, in so doing, making their lives, and yours, better for your efforts.

—John Lee Welton

ONE-ACT PLAYS

Listen to Me—Please
by Tom Smoot

(For youth)

Characters: 3 males, 2 females

(Song—"Lonely Voices," No. 63, Sing and Celebrate II, 1975) (During the song the four actors, except for the girl, take their place in a triangle, their backs to the audience. After they freeze in position, Cathy comes in, walks across stage and, not noticing the others, freezes until song is over. A red light is in her area at all times.)

GIRL: Have you ever been in a crowd, and felt alone? Have you sat at a ball game, been in a large shopping center, or sat in church, and still—been—alone? I have. My name is Cathy. I'm 17 and I won't be any older than 17—on this earth anyway. But I'll tell you about that later.

I grew up like most of you. Our family lived in a nice subdivision. There were plenty of children to play with in our neighborhood. I knew all of them by name. But I'm not sure if they knew my name or not. That's kind of the story of my life. I knew a lot of people in high school, too. I think I even had some friends, at least I talked to them in the auditorium and the cafeteria. But I was still lonely. Do you have friends, and yet feel lonely? I often heard our preacher in church say that—"Jesus" was a person who could be a friend, a friend who would never forsake you, or leave you— *ALONE.* I've wondered about that—but now I'll never find out, will I? And many people and quote friends and even my family had the chance to tell me. I never tried to push myself on any of them. I'm sure I gave them the chance. I never did anything to hurt them or give them a reason not to like me or accept me. I always thought I was just like one of the group, but I always seemed alone, among many people.

(Red light fades as spot comes up on Mother. As spot reaches full, Cathy should walk into the scene as Mother turns and speaks.)

MOTHER: Cathy, where have you been?

CATHY: I missed the bus at school, Mom, so I just walked home.

MOTHER: Sure you did. You've probably been riding around with those crazy kids from school.

CATHY: That's not right. I walked home by myself. I never go riding with them.

MOTHER: Well, your sister Jane has been home an hour, and she's already cleaned half the house.

CATHY: I'm sorry, Mom.

MOTHER: Sure, you're always sorry. But you *never* get here in time to help.

CATHY: I'm here now, maybe I can help you with supper.

7

MOTHER: Now what could you do in helping with supper? Anyway, Jane is going to cook supper tonight. She's going to try out a new recipe. Besides, you don't even know how to cook that well.

CATHY: That's because you taught her, and never bothered to teach me.

MOTHER: That's enough, Cathy!

CATHY: It seems to me she's always been the one who's gotten most of the attention around here the past few years.

MOTHER: Now don't get sassy with me, young lady. All you ever want to do is come home, and go to your room and close the door.

CATHY: It's my room, isn't it?

MOTHER: I don't know what you do up there, but it seems to me you're caught up in your own little world, and no one else is a part of it.

CATHY: Well, maybe that's because no one around here seems to care what I do, or what I don't do.

MOTHER: Now, that's about enough back talk. Maybe you ought to just *go* to your room, and your dad will deal with you when he gets home.

CATHY: Yeah, I wish he would. *(Starts to leave)*

MOTHER: And see if you can't take a few lessons from your sister on how to be a young lady.

(Lights fade as Cathy walks out of scene. Two lines of "Lonely Voices" play as Cathy walks toward Pastor. Lights come up on Pastor as Cathy walks into the scene. When she speaks, Pastor turns to respond.)

CATHY: Excuse me, Pastor, I wonder if I could talk with you for a minute.

PASTOR: Sure, I guess I have a few minutes before I have to go to the sanctuary.

CATHY: I was wondering . . .

PASTOR: Don't I know you? Let's see . . . now don't tell me. *(Pause)* Yes, aren't you one of the Simpson girls?

CATHY: Yes, I'm Cathy.

PASTOR: That's right. How are your parents, and your sister Jane?

CATHY: They're fine, I guess. You see, I . . .

PASTOR: That sister of yours, she is really a worker around here. She's done a great job on our youth committee. She also does a lot of work with our older folks. They really think a lot of her.

CATHY: Yes. I hear that all the time. That's what I want to talk to you about.

PASTOR: Oh. You want to become more involved in our church activities?

CATHY: Well, I think I need to talk to you about . . .

PASTOR: What all would be involved in it? Well, that really depends on what you put into it. You see . . .

CATHY: What I really need to know is why all these other kids around here aren't friendly?

PASTOR: That's just your imagination.

CATHY: Why don't they want me to get involved in their group?

PASTOR: I think *all* the youth around here are friendly.

CATHY: I can't seem to make friends with any of them. I really try. I do.

PASTOR: We teach and preach friendship here at our church. I try to teach our entire church of the kind of *friend* Jesus was. We encourage all our congregation to follow in His footsteps when He walked on this earth. I don't see *how*

8

you can say they're not friendly! Even our visitors speak about how friendly we are.

CATHY: But I always seem to be left out of everything.

PASTOR: Maybe if you would come to church more often, and do a little work around here, like your sister, you would feel more a part of the group!

CATHY: But I'm not Jane, and I do not want to be like her! I'm supposed to be Cathy, and accepted by others to be myself. Don't you teach that too? I want to know why I can't become a part of this church. I want to know of this friendship you talk about that Jesus has to offer. Can you tell me how I can experience it? That's what I want.

PASTOR: It *is* time for church to start. I've got to go now. Think about what I've said. Try to be more like Jane, and maybe you'll find that friendship you're looking for.

(Lights fade out as two lines of "Lonely Voices" *are sung. Cathy walks toward Bill. Lights up on Bill as Cathy walks into scene.)*

CATHY: Hello Bill.

BILL: Oh, hi Cathy. How are you?

CATHY: Okay, I guess.

BILL: Down again?

CATHY: Yes!

BILL: What's the matter this time? Things not been going well for you in our math class?

CATHY: No, that's not it.

BILL: Well, what's up?

CATHY: I don't know. It's probably just me, but I can't seem to find anyone I can really call a friend.

BILL: Oh, that's ridiculous. You know we all are your friends. What about all the people at Juanita's party the other night? Didn't you have a good time there? Everyone else did.

CATHY: I didn't go. I wasn't invited.

BILL: Oh? I thought I saw you there. Well maybe she thought Jane would bring you with her. I am sure that's it. Did Jane say anything to you about it?

CATHY: No. She just asked if I was invited and I said no, and she said that's too bad, that it was going to be a fun time.

BILL: Well, listen. Let me *personally* invite you to come to our Sunday School's hayride this Friday night. It'll be a good time, and I'm sure you'll see how many of our group can really be your friends.

CATHY: That sounds like fun.

BILL: Well, good. Just get a ride down to the church around 6:00. I'd come by and get you, but I already have four in the VW, and it gets a little crowded after that. I'm sure you can find someone to come pick you up.

CATHY: Who?

BILL: I don't know. Ask somebody. Listen, I've got to go now, the others are waiting to go over to Becky's house for a while, so if you can come, I'll see you at the hayride.

CATHY: Sure.

(Lights fade out as two lines of "Lonely Voices" *are sung. Cathy walks toward Jane. Lights up on Jane as Cathy walks into scene.)*

JANE: Oh, hello, Sis.

CATHY: Hi. What are you doing all dressed up?

JANE: I'm going to homecoming to-night, remember?

CATHY: Oh, yeah.

JANE: Aren't you going?

CATHY: You know I'm not.

JANE: Yes, I guess I did.

CATHY: You just thought you would rub it in, didn't you?

JANE: Now, that's not true, Cathy. You could go if you wanted to.

CATHY: Sure, by myself.

JANE: Oh, I'm sure someone would take you. Say, would you like me to find a date for you?

CATHY: No, thanks! You do enough for me already!

JANE: Well, I try to be the best sister I can.

CATHY: That's right, Jane. You're the best at everything.

JANE: Now I wouldn't go so far as to say that, Cathy.

CATHY: Sure you would.

JANE: Cathy.

CATHY: You're the best student, the best friend, the best cheerleader, the best youth at the church, even the best daughter at home.

JANE: That's all your imagination.

CATHY: Sure.

JANE: If you would just try you would be popular too. You're not going to get anywhere in life just being the little backward girl you appear to be to everybody.

CATHY: I don't want to be that popular; I just want to be liked for who I am.

JANE: If you want to be liked for who you are, you need to change who you are.

CATHY: That's just it. I don't want to change.

JANE: You better think about it real good, Cathy, if you want to get anything at all out of life.

(Lights fade out. Red light comes back up on stool. Cathy makes her way to the stool before she speaks.)

CATHY: I had cried out, but no one had heard. I showed up at parties to make friends, but it didn't seem to help. I didn't push myself on anyone. I wasn't outgoing like some of my classmates. I wasn't a cheerleader or even a class leader. Just a follower, I guess, but I wanted them, as *close* friends.

I had as much right as all the rest of them to be liked. I would have given anything to be popular, I just didn't know how.

It was the same at church as it was at school. The Pastor always talking about how friendly our little church was. That it was the place that I could find "Real Christian Friends."

I didn't know what it meant to be a real Christian, but I knew the word *friend*. And *that*—I wanted, and needed. And for the years I went to church, I don't know if anyone bothered to tell me what it meant to be a Christian. Oh, I'm sure they spoke about it in very general terms, but they didn't single me out, and tell me. It's not that I think I deserve special attention or anything. They all just seemed so impersonal about it. I wanted someone to tell *me* about this man Jesus, the One they say would *never* leave me *lonely*.

But it's too late now. *(Long pause)* You know the night of the church hayride Bill talked about? Well, I *was* going. I finally got a ride with a couple of others. We missed the truck before it left the church, but one of the girls knew where it was going. We were trying to catch up with it on this country road. At one place, the road curved sharply to the right, our car didn't. All three were pronounced "dead on arrival" at General Hospital. *(Pause)* Now it's too late—I'm still alone, wondering what it would have been like to live in a world with people, to get to know them and have them know me as a *person*; to be *one* of the group, to be a part of and not apart from. I also wonder what it would be like to know Jesus, a true friend. Why didn't they tell me? *(Freezes)*

(Lights come up on Mother. She turns and speaks directly to the audience.)

MOTHER: I couldn't believe it when I got the call from the hospital. My daughter, my baby, dead. I was going to make her stay home that night because Jane was having some friends over, and I knew I could get her to help with cleaning up afterwards. But she wanted to go so badly. *(Pause)* I knew I shouldn't have let her go. Why didn't she just decide to stay in her room like she did most of the time. She was never where she should have been. If I would have just had more time to work with her. There never seemed to be any time left. After all the work at church, and my work around here, and helping Jane with all her activities . . . there just wasn't enough time left. If only she could have been more like Jane! *(Lights fade on her.)*

(Lights up on pastor. He turns to the audience and speaks.)

PASTOR: You know, it's always a tragedy to see the loss of lives of our young people today. Whether we knew them very well or not, it's always a tragedy. I really didn't get to know Cathy very well. It's hard for me to get to know all the members of our congregation personally, especially the young people. I've spoken at a couple of their retreats in the past few years, but there just isn't enough time. I really feel sorry for her family. They're taking it pretty hard. But our entire congregation is ministering to them. It's remarkable how our church family helps me out in times of crisis. You know, as I reflect on my conversation with Cathy, she was having problems with friendships. If she could just see the friendliness of these people now, during this time of crisis.

I've assured her family that God will take care of her now. I looked on our church records, and she committed her life to Christ and was baptized when she was nine years old. I know that's a comfort to her family. I wish she could have realized that we are a friendly congregation, and that she could have known the relationship of Christ as a friend to her. If she would have just come around the church more often . . .

(Lights fade on pastor. Light up on Bill. He turns to the audience.)

BILL: I really don't know what to say. I guess we thought Cathy was involved in most of the things we were. I don't imagine any of us really made a special effort to invite her to go places with us. We don't really play favorites. I don't know if she thought we should have treated her any differently or special than we would treat anyone else. She was invited along with everyone else to our parties. If she didn't get an invitation, she could have come anyway. It's usually no big thing. She seemed as if she wanted to be alone. And if someone wants to be alone, you should let them be alone, right?

I guess the really sad thing is that even though I know Jane is a good Christian, I'm not sure about Cathy. I guess we all thought she was. But if we were really her friends, we should have known. I guess the saddest part of all of this is that *I* didn't know whether she was a Christian or not. If I was her friend I really should have known. I'm sorry, Cathy. I really am. Can you hear me? I'm sorry. *(Lights fade on Bill. Light up on Jane. She speaks to the audience.)*

JANE: *(Sadly)* Best student, best friend, best youth at church, and even the best daughter. Right now, I sure wish I could add "best sister." I could see what was going on in Cathy's life. I really could. I could see the favors from Mom and Dad always seeming to come my way. At times, I wanted to say something to them about it, but just never did. I wish I had. I tried to be sensitive to Cathy's feelings of rejection. She really never gave me a chance. To her, it was always *my fault* that I was popular, or looked at as a leader. It really wasn't. I just seemed to be able to "fall into place" better than she. Can that be totally my fault? I feel so sorry for Mom and Dad. They're really taking it hard. I guess where I really failed was that I was only being *sensitive* to her feelings, and not actually responding to her real needs. I'm sorry she felt the way she did about me. It wasn't all my fault. I guess we really needed to give each other a chance. *(Lights fade on Jane and the red light comes up on Cathy, who has been by the stool during these monologues.)*

CATHY: They're all too late now. They wanted me to know, they wanted me to be a part of them, but nothing was ever done about it. I didn't choose to be a loner. They all had a chance to take me in, to accept me, to make me a part of their lives—and I was willing. You know, they just never asked me. That's all they had to do, just ask. I was there, and willing. I hope there are no more Cathy Simpson's in the world, going unnoticed, because no one really took time to be their friend. You won't let that happen, will you?

(This Scripture should be read as music to "Lonely Voices" plays in the background. Then bring up music louder as the three actors leave stage. Cathy should remain on stage sitting on a stool as the red light slowly fades.)

"Listen to my prayer, O God; don't hide yourself when I cry to you. Hear me, Lord! Listen to me!" *(Ps. 55:1, TLB)*

Unclean
by Rod Payne

(Discussion Drama)

Cast: Mrs. Elms, Mrs. Simms, Preacher Miller, Mrs. Lawrence, Man in the Audience, Companion (no lines)

Scene One

Setting: An office area in a small church. Two women are seated at a table; they are calculating the Sunday School reports.

MRS. ELMS: I just don't know why they have to have separate forms for the first and second grades. They only have

12

two children in each grade.

MRS. SIMMS: It's something about keeping track of the total number of kids going to church in all Southern Baptist churches in the country. You know, we send all this information into the state office and they send it to Nashville, or something like that.

MRS. ELMS: Well, I don't know about all that, but I do know they could probably save a lot of money if they didn't have all of these forms. What's this? (*She holds up an offering envelope and tries to open it.*)

MRS. SIMMS: Let me see it. (*She takes the envelope and tries in vain to open it. Holding it before her she reads the name on the envelope.*) Bobby Miller. Wait, there's something written on the back. (*Reads from back of envelope.*) "This is God's money so keep your hands off of it." (*She holds the envelope to her nose and sniffs of the outside.*) He's glued this thing together.

(*Preacher Miller approaches the women from behind.*)

MRS. ELMS: That Bobby Miller. Well, you know what they say about preacher's kids.

MILLER: No, what do that say about preacher's kids?

MRS. ELMS: (*Startled*) Oh, Brother Miller, I didn't see you there.

MILLER: (*Walks around table to face women. He smiles.*) I see you got my son's sealed envelope. He told me he was going to figure out a way to make sure all of his money got into the right hands.

MRS. SIMMS: Well, he certainly knows how to get his point across.

MILLER: There are times I wish he'd pass on some of that talent to me, like when I'm preaching. (*He looks through the papers on the table.*) So, how many did we have in Sunday School this morning?

MRS. ELMS: Forty-five, counting the Pinson baby.

MILLER: That's about normal for us. Have you got the list of the missing members together yet?

MRS. SIMMS: It's right here; I was just finishing it. The Edwards family isn't here today, Brother Miller. Have you heard anything about them?

MILLER: I've heard they were taking their son to the doctor this week, but I didn't catch what it was they were having him treated for.

MRS. ELMS: Eric has had problems ever since the accident.

MRS. SIMMS: I didn't know he had been hurt that badly.

MILLER: He did lose a little blood before the doctors could get his arm sewn up. I think they had to give him a pint or two. It just goes to show that kids really can get hurt on those skateboards.

MRS. LAWRENCE: (*Entering*) Oh, Brother Miller, I was just looking for you. I want to know if what I've heard is true and if it is, what are you going to do about it?

MILLER: I'm afraid you have the advantage of me, Mrs. Lawrence, in that I don't know what you've heard.

MRS. LAWRENCE: It's about the Edwards boy. I thought you must have already heard about it or I wouldn't be asking you. (*She looks at the other two women in the room.*) You haven't heard about it either?

MRS. SIMMS: (*Drawing her chair closer to Mrs. Lawrence*) No, we haven't heard anything. We knew they were absent this morning and the pastor was telling us they had to take their son to the doctor last week.

MILLER: Have you heard some word about the boy, Mrs. Lawrence?

MRS. LAWRENCE: Yes. My daughter hangs around with Melisa Robbins and Melisa works two hours a day in the office at school. You know, she takes phone messages and runs errands for the teachers. Anyway, Melisa told my daughter she overheard the school counselor talking to Mrs. Edwards on the phone late last week. They were talking about Eric. They were discussing whether or not Eric would be allowed to come back to school because he's got AIDS.

MILLER: Are you sure, Mrs. Lawrence? Maybe this is some kind of school girl's prank. This Melisa may have told your daughter a story, just to see what her reaction would be or something like that.

MRS. LAWRENCE: No, that's not the case. Eric wasn't at school on Friday. Melisa told my daughter that the school's attorney came to the school on Friday morning and there were several members of the school board there, too.

MILLER: Be that as it may, Mrs. Lawrence, we don't really know if Eric Edwards has AIDS and even if he does we don't know how that's going to impact our church.

MRS. LAWRENCE: I can tell you one thing, that child shouldn't be allowed in the building with the other children.

They don't have a cure for AIDS and there's no reason to expose children here at church to it. For heaven's sake; they won't even let him go to school.

MRS. SIMMS: I've heard you can get it just from being in the same room with those people.

MRS. ELMS: Isn't it awful! I wonder how the boy caught it?

MRS. LAWRENCE: Well, I don't know, but the important thing is not letting anybody else in the church catch it from him. That's why I came to see you, Brother Miller. I wanted to know what you planned to do about it. Are you going to let them bring their son back here to the church?

MILLER: Now, Mrs. Lawrence, I don't think it's fair to ask me what I am going to do right now. In the first place, this kind of thing needs to be discussed before the entire church. That's if there really is any truth to it at all.

MRS. LAWRENCE: I've known Melisa Robbins for years and I know she wouldn't lie about something like this.

MRS. SIMMS: She's always seemed like such a nice girl.

(*Mrs. Elms nods in agreement and the three women turn to look at Miller.*)

MILLER: Well, we'll just have to approach this thing delicately. This kind of matter may not even be one which should be discussed before the whole church—now that I think about it.

MRS. LAWRENCE: I don't know what you mean, Brother Miller. AIDS kills; even my five-year-old can tell you that. People with AIDS can cause other people to get it. We've got to act now. I'm not just thinking of us. (*Gestures around* *the room*.) I'm also thinking of the Edwards family.

MRS. SIMMS: I know what she's trying to say. You need to talk to them before they try to come back so it won't be so embarrassing for them. Surely they won't want to have their son return to Sunday School or anything.

MRS. ELMS: That's probably true. It's so sad about the boy, though. Well, who knows what's going to happen next? Anyway, we have to take these reports out to be posted.

MRS. SIMMS: (*Leaving with Mrs. Elms*) I've heard you can even catch it from drinking from the same water fountain.

MRS. LAWRENCE: I know how you feel, Brother Miller. It's a difficult situation, but you have to think of the whole church and not just one family.

MILLER: It's not that so much; I'm concerned about the Edwards and how they must be feeling. They may have stayed home from church today because they were worried about how people here would react to them and to their son. They may need us right now and we don't even know it.

MRS. LAWRENCE: That may be true, but if I were you I'd call them. I wouldn't go over there. You've got your family to think about, let alone this church. This is something you can't help.

MILLER: But maybe we can help. If their son really does have AIDS, they need our support; (*Pause*) they need our prayers.

MRS. LAWRENCE: I'm not saying they don't. You could still—*we* could

still, help them. But we've got to be realistic about this, too. Maybe you could send a tape of the services to their house, like you do for some of the shut-ins. We could get some of the ladies in the church to make food for them.

MILLER: Oh, and how will the Edwards get it? Will you arrange a drop-off somewhere in the park? That way you won't have to get near them.

MRS. LAWRENCE: There's no need to get upset with me. I'm not the one who has AIDS. I'm just trying to help, that's all.

(*A commotion has started in the audience. It appears two people are arguing, with one of the pair becoming louder and louder. The other person is trying to quiet his companion down. This activity should begin at this point and gradually increase until the point that it is brought to the fore of the audience's attention.*)

MILLER: (*Continues. He does not seem to notice what is happening in the audience.*) I know you are, Mrs. Lawrence, but I just think we need to be a little more concerned about the Edwards family. After all, the church is the first place people ought to be able to turn to when they're having trouble.

(*The noise in the audience is growing louder. One of the men is pointing at the stage and shaking his head.*)

MRS. LAWRENCE: (*She does not appear to notice the commotion in the audience.*) Sure, people ought to be able to turn to the church, but the church has to be able to protect itself, too.

MAN IN THE AUDIENCE: (*This is the man who has been pointing his finger and arguing with his companion. He now* rises in the audience and begins to shout at the actors on stage.) To protect itself! You're saying the church ought to be allowed to protect itself? I can't believe you're saying that.

(*His companion tries to pull the man back into his seat, but the man violently pushes him away. The man begins to move toward the stage area.*)

MAN: Unclean! Unclean!

MILLER: (*Confused, dropping character. All lines from this point must be very realistic and not "acted." Looking toward the audience*) What's going on out there?

MAN: (*Continuing to move toward the stage*) Unclean! Unclean!

MILLER: (*Looks to the side of the stage.*) Can't you do something about this? (*Turns and looks back at the man who is still moving toward the stage.*) What do you want?

MAN: Unclean! Unclean! (*The man stops before he actually reaches the two actors on stage.*) Unclean! Unclean! (*He turns and looks at the audience.*)

MRS. LAWRENCE: You'd probably better leave him alone. He's acting like he's crazy.

MAN: (*Turning back to the actors on stage*) Crazy? No, lady, I'm not crazy; I'm infected.

MRS. LAWRENCE: (*She has placed the table between herself and the edge of the stage.*) Please sit down, sir, and let us finish our play.

MAN: You are finished. Don't you get it?

MILLER: Sir, really, just take a seat. I'm sure someone will be here to help you pretty quickly.

MAN: I don't want to sit down. I'll guarantee you, though, I could sit anywhere in here and people would move out for me.

MILLER: I'm sure that's true. In fact, there's a good seat right over there. If you'll just sit down . . .

MAN: Unclean! Unclean! (*He turns and shouts at the audience.*) Unclean! Unclean!

MILLER: Now look here; this has got to stop! (*He moves toward the edge of the stage, closer to the man.*)

MAN: Don't come another step closer. (*To audience*) Don't any of you come another step closer. I've got it and if you get close to me you might catch it.

MILLER: You've got what?

MAN: AIDS! Don't you understand? I have the very thing you're trying to protect yourself against. Me, right here in this body. Something is going through me which is going to kill me before long and the doctors don't even know how to stop it. I'm unclean, to hear her tell it. (*Man points at Mrs. Lawrence.*)

MILLER: No, you've got it all wrong. This is just a play. We're just trying to communicate an idea about a very real problem.

MAN: Well, this is as real as it gets. You're sitting up there talking about how to handle a person with AIDS and I'm giving you the opportunity to try your hand on the real thing.

MILLER: Sir, really, if you'll just sit down. We can talk after the program is over. I want to talk to you; in fact I'm sure there are several people here who would talk with you after the program.

MRS. LAWRENCE: I don't know

what's going on here but I'm leaving. I'll be backstage if you get this straightened out. (*Mrs. Lawrence starts to exit the stage.*)

MAN: Sure, go ahead; that's the best way to solve your problems. Go ahead, leave; that'll take care of everything. Then you won't have to face me or worry about my problems.

MRS. LAWRENCE: Look, for all I know you could be crazy and actually have AIDS. All I do know is I didn't come here to take part in anything like this.

MILLER: It's okay. Why don't you just, uh, go backstage for a few minutes. I'm sure we can work something out. I must apologize to our audience. Maybe we could take a short break in the program while we attend to this man.

MAN: No break, no break. I haven't been able to get a break; why should you have one?

(*Mrs. Lawrence stays on stage but continues to keep the table between herself and the Man in the Audience.*)

MILLER: Look, sir, what is it, exactly, that you want?

MRS. LAWRENCE: Yes, maybe if you could tell us what you want we could help you or . . .

MAN: Just a second; I was watching this little play and I saw how you wanted to help *that* family. You wanted to give them whatever you could as long as you could do it by long distance. Sure, send your tax deductible donations in and you'll never have to see the poor unfortunates who really need your help. Compassion by proxy. (*Man moves to be seated on the side of the stage area. As he does*

both Miller and Mrs. Lawrence take a few steps back as if to maintain distance between themselves and the Man.)

MILLER: That wasn't the point of the play at all.

MRS. LAWRENCE: If you would have let us finish you might have been surprised by the outcome.

MAN: Why don't you surprise me in person? You don't have to pretend with me. (*Man turns back to audience.*) Stay back all of you.

MILLER: No one is going to bother you, Mister. Uh, what is your name?

MAN: Never mind that, unless you want to contribute to my headstone fund. I'm not going to be around long enough for you to get to know me. Even if you did, that wouldn't matter; not really.

MILLER: (*Moving closer to Man*) What does matter? I mean, what really matters to you?

MRS. LAWRENCE: Don't get too close; if he really is carrying AIDS you don't know what could happen.

MAN: Oh, lady, how wrong you are. You *can* be sure of two things about me; I will die from this disease and I will probably die alone.

MILLER: What about your family? Don't they care about you?

MAN: Oh, sure, I guess they care, but they're just like you in a way. They want to care, but they don't want to get too close. I don't blame them, really. I must've done something wrong; must've committed some special sin, to have caused me to catch it. It's a curse from God, right?

MILLER: I've heard it described like that. I don't know, maybe it is.

MAN: (*Starting to calm down*) That's what all you people say. Everyone of you believe AIDS is a curse from God. It's a curse sent to punish someone or something bad.

MRS. LAWRENCE: Curse or not I'll bet it's cut down on the amount of sex outside of marriage. That's worth something.

MAN: I guess, then, my death will mean something. After all, according to you I'll be dying to keep this country clean.

MILLER: (*Walks away to the far side of the stage as he speaks.*) No, I don't believe it's just that. I think God may have allowed this to happen, but I don't think He ever wants innocent people to suffer.

MRS. LAWRENCE: But AIDS isn't going to bother someone who's innocent. It's only going to affect those people like, well, you know.

MAN: Yeah, I know, people *like me.* Lady, what you don't know I don't have time to tell you. Hey, preacher, wasn't there supposed to be some deal in the Bible about getting forgiven or something? Maybe that would work.

MILLER: What do you mean?

MAN: If God really did let this happen to me because He was mad about something, then maybe if He forgave me I'd get over it. You know, something like a commuted sentence. I could trade AIDS for something like cancer.

MILLER: God doesn't operate that way. He's already commuted our death sentence by sending His Son to die for us. As to your forgiveness, all you have to do is ask Him.

MAN: That's great, really. If I understand you right all I have to do to get His forgiveness is ask and then He'll take care of this sickness in me.

MRS. LAWRENCE: You can't be serious. I'm no biblical scholar but I can tell you there's nothing in the Bible that says God will save you from a curse He's put on you.

MILLER: Wait just a second. We really don't know if this disease is a curse from God in the first place, and in the second place, there is biblical evidence of God withholding His anger from His people when they've repented.

MAN: That settles it for me. (*Looks up.*) God, I'm sorry for whatever it was I did that made You so mad at me. Let's just start fresh from right now. (*Man looks at his hands and then examines the rest of himself.*) That's odd, I don't feel or look any different. Hey, what is this? I don't think anything happened at all.

MILLER: Did you really mean it?

MAN: What do you mean, did I really mean it? Wouldn't you? Of course I meant I don't want to have AIDS anymore!

MILLER: No, I didn't mean that. I know you don't want the AIDS virus; I meant did you really mean it when you told God you were sorry?

MAN: What business is that of yours? A man's relationship with God should be private.

MRS. LAWRENCE: You can't reason with this man. Why are we even letting him disrupt the program like this?

MILLER: That's not the point. That hasn't been the point the whole time. He's right, you know. We were supposed to be up here showing how the church can deal with the AIDS crisis and, when it comes down to it, I think we may have missed the whole point in our rush to climb on some sort of "vengeance is mine" bandwagon.

MRS. LAWRENCE: I'm sorry for him, honestly. It's just that so many people bring this on themselves.

MAN: Yeah, you're probably right. I guess some sort of divine healing would be out, too. I mean you guys don't even believe in that kind of thing.

MILLER: No, that's not it, either. We do believe in God's power to heal and I'm not saying that won't happen in your case. But that's still not the point. That word you were shouting when you started up here, *unclean*, that's the real point.

MAN: Oh, I get it. The real point goes back to the protection bit, right? You've got to protect yourself from people like me and if and when God ever sees fit to give me a break, then I'm to report to you. Then you'll be ready to help me out. Great.

MILLER: No. (*Turning to Mrs. Lawrence*) Don't you see? It's just like the lepers in the Bible.

MRS. LAWRENCE: But it's not the same. For all we know those were innocent men who just contracted some sort (*Begins to slow down on each of the last two words as she comes to a conclusion*) of . . . disease. (*Sits*) But we know all kinds of prostitutes and homosexuals are getting AIDS.

MAN: I'm not a homosexual!

MILLER: But we also know innocent people who are suffering because of it, people who caught it through no fault of their own. But there's a bigger issue here.

MAN: If it's any bigger than death I don't want to know about it.

MILLER: (*Sits on the apron of the stage beside the Man.*) The issue isn't whether or not God's going to cure you of AIDS because He has the power to do anything He wants to. The real issue here is how you're going to respond to God.

MAN: Oh, I thought . . .

MILLER: And really that's only part of the issue. We've also got to figure out how we're going to respond to you.

MAN: I think she's got that part figured out.

MRS. LAWRENCE: Wait a minute. I was just saying the lines the author gave me up here.

MAN: Yeah, but you said them like you believed them.

MILLER: Maybe that's all I've been doing in my own Christian walk, repeating the lines I've heard without really believing them— stuff like, "inasmuch as ye have done it unto one of the least of these" (*Matt. 25:40, KJV*) and all those promises of protection the Bible offers.

MAN: Protection? What protection? Get real.

MILLER: No, really. God offers His protection to people who are doing His will. He says so. We've got to believe that or we'd be afraid to try anything in His name. Yet we continue to branch out and form new churches.

MAN: That's all well and good, but all those churches mean to me is just more doors for people to hide behind.

MILLER: Maybe, or they could be more doors for you to come inside. They could be more doors for us to leave from as we go out and look for people like you, people who need our help.

MAN: I don't know if you've got any help for me anyway.

MILLER: We (*Indicates Mrs. Lawrence and himself.*) can introduce you to someone who does. If you really want to talk to God, He's right here with us right now. I can't promise He'll heal you, but I can tell you He's healed others.

MRS. LAWRENCE: He promises forgiveness if we just ask Him.

MAN: And what do I need to be forgiven for? I'm the one He made sick. It should be Him asking me for forgiveness!

MILLER: No, that's not true. Whatever has happened, God doesn't owe any man an apology. We're the ones who broke His heart with our sin. I know it's easy for me to say because I'm not the one with AIDS. But God doesn't have to have our forgiveness; we have to have His. Look, even if you didn't do anything to bring this disease on yourself, the root cause for the spread of AIDS is still sin. Whether it's sex or drugs it's still sin to God.

MAN: Here we go with the sermon. Look, I don't need sermons. (*Man rises and starts to leave.*) I don't even know why I came here in the first place. I don't need you and you don't want to have anything to do with me.

MRS. LAWRENCE: Wait, don't leave! God won't let me let you leave.

MAN: Lady, there's nothing you can do to stop me. I don't need any more of your condemnation. God's already shown me what He thinks of me and I'll die from it soon enough.

MRS. LAWRENCE: If AIDS really is God's death sentence then I deserve to die by it, too. I should be standing right where you're standing. Sin is sin to God and He promises death as the final payment for sin. (*Walks toward Man who looks puzzled.*) Don't you see? I don't know whether AIDS is God's death sentence or just the natural outcome of sin, but I do know this; I've sinned and He's forgiven me.

MAN: Good for Him and good for you.

MRS. LAWRENCE: I want you to know that same forgiveness. I don't think I can really accept forgiveness for my sin if I let you walk out of here without trying to help you.

MAN: What?

MILLER: I'm beginning to understand.

MAN: Great. You two just talk among yourselves; I've had enough with all of this stuff.

MILLER: She's right; we can't let you go. I mean we're not going to hold you here by force or anything like that. It's just that we've been given something and that something came with instructions.

MAN: Look, (*Pointing to Miller*) you're making even less sense than she is.

MRS. LAWRENCE: I was wrong, all right? I was wrong to say the things I said. I was just afraid, that's all. This AIDS thing is so deadly, so final, and so unknown. But that doesn't excuse me from my duty.

MAN: I don't want to put you out, lady, really. You're under no obligation.

MILLER: Yes, we are. We're under a direct command. We don't owe you; we owe God. We owe Him our lives and our love and He's told us to share both with other people.

MAN: Kind of like an "adopt an AIDS victim" week, right?

MRS. LAWRENCE: (*Walking toward Man*) It's more a matter of showing the same kind of "love you've been shown" week. I don't blame you for thinking we're not serious, but we are. God wants me to show you the same kind of love He's shown me. I've got to do it.

MILLER: *We've* got to do it.

MAN: Well, that'll be nice for today. Come tomorrow, though, I'll be too inconvenient for you to mess with.

MRS. LAWRENCE: I don't expect you to believe me right now, but that's not going to happen.

MILLER: God won't abandon us and we can't abandon you.

MRS. LAWRENCE: You can trust Him right now and we'll just have to earn your trust.

MAN: I don't know.

MILLER: Look, let's get out of here and go some place where we can talk without all these people. If you want to pray we'll help you. (*Moves to Man and reaches out his hand. Man starts to reach for Miller's hand then draws back his own. Mrs. Lawrence moves between them and takes both their hands.*)

MRS. LAWRENCE: C'mon you two. These people probably want to get on with their meeting. They've got all kinds of reports and things to look at, you know, church business.

(*The trio exit the auditorium.*)

The Riverfront Cafe
by Matthew Trent Tullos

(Valentine's program, dinner theater, family relations program)

Characters: 1 male, 1 female

Scene One

Setting: The stage is set with two chairs and a table decorated with a modest tablecloth, two candles, and menus. Each piece should have a timeless countenance to allow set changes between scenes to be minimal.

(*Lights fade up. Gladys is sitting in one of the chairs at the table looking at the menu. Joe enters stage right. He is not seen nor heard by Gladys.*)

JOE: (*To himself, trying to sound reassured*) Here it is—the Riverfront Cafe. I know—it's not French cuisine with silk tableclothes and finely crafted silverware, but they make great spaghetti. (*Joe strides over to the table.*)

JOE: Hi, Gladys. Sorry I'm late. (*They embrace.*)

GLADYS: I was getting a little worried.

JOE: It's just that today is such an important day.

GLADYS: What's important?

JOE: Don't get ahead of me. It's a surprise. (*Looking to an imaginary waiter and menu*) I'll have the spaghetti.

GLADYS: Me too. (*Pause*)

JOE: Ice tea.

GLADYS: Me too. (*Pause*)

JOE: No, thanks. That's all. Anything else for you?

GLADYS: (*Gladys shakes her head no.*)

JOE: Thanks. (*Pause*) He's new here, isn't he?

GLADYS: Yeah—His name is

Henderson.

JOE: What's his first name?

GLADYS: That is his first name. Now, what makes this such an important day?

JOE: Do you want the long version or the short version?

GLADYS: Better give me the long one.

JOE: Okay *(Takes a breath.)* I was reading the story of Abraham and Sarah last night.

GLADYS: *(Skeptical)* Does this have anything to do with theology?

JOE: Absolutely not.

GLADYS: Great.

JOE: Well, kind of—

GLADYS: Uh oh!

JOE: Anyway, I was really impressed with the amount of faith the man had. He did have his weak moments, but overall he was quite a godly man.

GLADYS: That's how he got in the book.

JOE: Right. We digress.

GLADYS: What happened next?

JOE: I fell asleep. *(Pause)*

GLADYS: That's all?

JOE: No. I fell asleep and dreamed that I was Abraham, and guess who was Sarah?

GLADYS: Who?

JOE: You.

(Gladys laughs.)

JOE: This is perfect. That's exactly what Sarah did when Abraham told her that she was going to have a child.

GLADYS: Don't stop. What happened next?

JOE: I woke up.

GLADYS: Oh.

JOE: That was all the proof I needed from the Lord. I realized that the rest

was up to me. So I left work early today to buy you this. *(He hands her a small gift.)*

GLADYS: Oh, Joe! What is it?

JOE: Don't open it yet. After that I spent the rest of my day trying to put my feelings down on paper. I'm no poet, but here goes . . .

Take my hand and come with me.
Our souls will lose all gravity.
Together we will share the sky.
We'll smile as shooting stars go by.
Our wings of faith in dreams come
true
Will curl around the "me and
you."
Let's leave this den of petty rage.
The world won't miss us for an
age.

GLADYS: Oh, that's sweet.

JOE: Thank you.

GLADYS: Strange but sweet.

JOE: Now you can open it.

(Gladys unwraps the present.)

GLADYS: *(Giggling at first)* This looks like an engagement ring. *(Change of emotion)* This is a joke, isn't it?

JOE: Nope.

GLADYS: Tell me this is a joke!

JOE: I can't. 'Cause it's not. *(Gladys is stunned.)* Well, what do you say? Will you marry me?

GLADYS: No! absolutely, positively, no!!

JOE: Are you sure?

GLADYS: Yes.

JOE: Yes—you will marry me?

GLADYS: No.

JOE: No—you're not sure?

GLADYS: Yes, I'm—No, I'm sure— I'm—*(Getting louder)* Listen. This is only the third . . .

JOE: People are staring at us.

GLADYS: *(Whispering)* This is only the third time we've been out together. We hardly know each other.

JOE: That can change.

GLADYS: Joe, Joe, Joe! The answer is No! No! No!

JOE: I know I'm not much of a persuasive person, but . . .

GLADYS: Who do you think we are? Romeo and Juliet?

JOE: No—just Joe and Gladys. Listen, will you just give it some thought?

GLADYS: What?

JOE: Sleep on it. And I'll give you a call in the morning . . . say 6:30?

GLADYS: Cancel my order—I'm suddenly not hungry. *(Gladys gets up from the table.)*

JOE: Gladys, you're being irrational.

GLADYS: Me? Irrational? *(Gladys leaves.)*

JOE: Hey! Where are you going—Wait up!

(Black out)

(In the darkness tape recording is played of Joe's voice.)

JOE'S VOICE: It didn't look good at that particular time. I was shocked by her shock. She was shocked that I was shocked by her shock. I didn't hear from Gladys for a couple of weeks. Then I received a card from her. It simply said, "Love is patient." I tried to master the art of patience, and three years later we were married. Not only were we married—we were married to each other!

Scene Two

(Joe and Gladys walk in. Joe is blindfolded. Gladys is guiding him on stage.)

GLADYS: Keep your eyes closed. Walk over here. Now, where are we?

JOE: The A&P.

GLADYS: No.

JOE: Your parents'.

GLADYS: No.

JOE: The bus station.

GLADYS: Joe, you're not even guessing! Why would I take you to the bus station?

JOE: Get rid of me, I guess. Can I take the blindfold off? This is getting embarrassing.

GLADYS: You're not playing fair. First guess.

JOE: The Riverfront Cafe, of course.

GLADYS: How did you know?

JOE: We always come here on special occasions.

GLADYS: How did you know this was a special occasion?

JOE: It's been a long time since I've had to wear a tie and a blindfold to dinner. *(Takes blindfold off.)*

JOE: So, what's the surprise?

GLADYS: It shouldn't be a surprise. Don't you remember what happened 10 years ago? *(Pause)* December 18, 1925.

JOE: How should I know? That was 10 years ago.

GLADYS: That's what I just said! Think, Joe!

(They sit.)

GLADYS: Maybe this will refresh your memory:

Take my hand and come with me.
Our souls will lose all gravity.
Together we will share the sky.
We'll smile as shooting stars go by.

JOE: Is that from an old boy friend?

GLADYS: An old lover.

JOE: What?

GLADYS: You!

JOE: I'm not *that* old.

GLADYS: Don't you remember, Joe? Ten years ago today, we were sitting in this very restaurant. I walked out on you after you proposed.

JOE: I remember. It took you three years to say yes.

GLADYS: We had a lot of differences to overcome.

JOE: I remember my dad saying, "You gonna marry a preacher's kid?"

GLADYS: It took a while, but you finally convinced me.

JOE: I sure am glad *those* days are over.

GLADYS: *Are* you?

JOE: Of course.

GLADYS: Do you ever regret it?

JOE: What are you talking about?

GLADYS: Do you ever regret marrying me?

JOE: No. What makes you ask?

GLADYS: Do you love me?

JOE: Gladys! What has gotten into you?

GLADYS: I just want to know.

JOE: What did I tell you yesterday?

GLADYS: When?

JOE: Right before I left for work.

GLADYS: That was four in the morning!

JOE: I told you that I loved you. And the day before that, and the day before that, and two years ago I was saying the same thing.

GLADYS: Look, Joe. I don't care if you told me two years ago or two hundred times yesterday! I need to know now! Do you love me now?

JOE: Yes! Yes! Yes! For crying out loud, what do you think I've been up to all these years?

GLADYS: I'm sorry. *(Almost crying)* I've just been kind of upset.

JOE: Kind of?

GLADYS: Just moody lately, I guess.

JOE: No kidding.

GLADYS: Eating like a pig.

JOE: Not that bad.

GLADYS: I'm gaining weight, Joe.

JOE: Glad, that's crazy. You're as skinny as a rail.

GLADYS: Joe, I went to the doctor.

JOE: Because you're gaining weight?

GLADYS: I'm expecting!

JOE: Right. *(Pause, then realized what she has just said.)* Expecting! Expecting a baby?

GLADYS: Yes. I found out today!

JOE: I can't believe it! I just can't believe it! We're gonna have a baby!

GLADYS: Are you happy?

JOE: Look at me! Look at you! Look at us! Us is three now. We've prayed for this moment for three years now. It's really going to happen. The Lord heard us. He answered our prayers.

(They spontaneously stand up and embrace.)

GLADYS: I'm so glad you're excited. I'm too excited to even think about it!

(They look around as if they are being stared at. Embarrassed, they break the embrace and address the patrons.)

GLADYS: Oh, please excuse us.

JOE: We're having a baby. *(Correcting himself)* Oh no, not at this moment. I mean I just found out that Gladys here is preg—I mean expecting. *(Pause—smiling as if he is receiving congratulations)* Thanks.

(Joe and Gladys return to seats at table. They clasp hands across the table.)

JOE: Thank You, Jesus. Thank You for this wonderful gift. All I can say is thank You. All we can do is thank You.
(Black out)
GLADYS' VOICE ON TAPE: Born on September 3, 1936, we named him Jonathan David. Times were hard, but we were very happy. Joe's job at the Williamsville Times provided a decent salary but very long hours. We were just so thankful that Joe had a job during the Depression. Soon after Jonathan was born, Joe was promoted to assistant editor. In 1940 Angela was born. The more, the merrier, we thought. And it was. But we also found out that "the more, the louder," and "the more, the messier," and of course, "the more, the busier." But every now and then, we made it out to the Riverfront Cafe.

Scene Three

(Lights up. Gladys and Joe are sitting at their table.)
JOE: Well . . . what about it?
GLADYS: I don't know. I've thought about it all week, and I can't think of any logical reason not to move.
JOE: It sure would be nice to have the extra money.
GLADYS: Chicago . . .
JOE: Big city.
GLADYS: There are so many things our kids could see and experience.
JOE: Good and bad. *(Pause)* The guys in the office think I'm crazy not to jump at the offer.
GLADYS: We could probably afford a larger house.
JOE: A new car.
GLADYS: Jonathan wanted to know last night if they had Sunday School in

Chicago. *(Pause)*
JOE: We've waited for this kind of thing to happen for years . . . haven't we?
GLADYS: I suppose.
JOE: It's the American dream—but is it our dream . . . climbing the salary ladder? Living in a big house that's just a little smaller than the one on the other side of the fence? You know, I bet thousands of people in Chicago would love to have a couple of acres in a town like Williamsville. Not a whole lot of money here but plenty of days. Days you just don't see in the city. Days to watch the kids grow up . . . days to weed the garden . . . hours to read and time to think. Time to get to know people, time to know God. Come to think of it, I'd trade steak in Chicago for grits in Williamsville anyday. *(Pause)* I'm sorry, Glad. I just don't feel like we need to leave. We've got a garden this year. Jonathan's just getting into the swing of school. *(Pause)* What are you smiling about?
GLADYS: I'm happy.
JOE: What?
GLADYS: I'm so thankful.
JOE: I thought you wanted to go.
GLADYS: I wanted to be excited with you. It was a great honor. The *Chicago Tribune* . . . you always talked about being a sports writer in a big city. I just left the whole thing for you and God to work out.
JOE: Me and God, huh?
GLADYS: Actually, it was *me* and God. I told God I didn't want to go.
JOE: *(Sarcastically)* Oh, great.
GLADYS: Just kidding.
JOE: Well, let's go pick up the kids from Mom and Dad's and watch the tomatoes

grow.

GLADYS: Joe! It's nine o'clock.

JOE: Okay, so we'll bring a flashlight.

(Black out)

JOE'S VOICE ON TAPE: Dear Gladys,

Something strange happened yesterday.

I looked into your eyes.

Five years danced by . . .

Your face showed little change.

Your eyes . . . your eyes had changed dramatically.

They stared so much further into mine.

They knew thoughts that burst from my single glance.

Ambition poured out of your eyes,

Driving me . . .

Pressing me . . .

Forward.

To be all that you dreamed we could be.

I glanced away from your eyes,

And when my eyes returned

A score of years had passed.

I saw those eyes deepen and expand . . .

They were the eyes of a woman

Whose courage flooded my very being.

Eyes that saw her children grow.

Eyes of shared joy.

Eyes of holy sacrifice.

Eyes of unbounded virtue.

Eyes that became a touchstone of womanhood.

I hear you say, "Why do you stare?"

This is why.

Scene Four

(Gladys and Joe stare in silence at each other. Finally Gladys speaks.)

GLADYS: Well?

JOE: What?

GLADYS: Didn't you—I mean, weren't you about to say something?

JOE: No.

GLADYS: Oh. *(Distantly pouting)*

JOE: What's the matter?

GLADYS: *(Defensively)* Nothing . . .

JOE: There is something wrong. I can tell by the way your voice trails up when you said "nothing." You say *(Imitating Gladys)* "nothing." You would have said *(Imitating sincerity)* "oh, nothing" if it were nothing, but you said *(Imitating Gladys)* "nothing." *(Pause)* Now, what's wrong?

GLADYS: *(Imitating sincerity)* Oh, nothing.

JOE: Now you're acting. You're a terrible actor. I can see right through it.

GLADYS: *(Sarcastically)* Thanks, Joe. Thank you very much.

JOE: *(Sincerely)* I'm sorry.

GLADYS: You really know how to show a girl a good time.

JOE: Have for 25 years.

GLADYS: For 25 years we've been having this conversation. *(Pause)* Sometimes it seems like you know everything there is to know about me. You've heard all my stories, and I've heard all yours. What else is there to talk about?

JOE: You haven't heard all my stories.

GLADYS: Have too!

JOE: Have not. What makes you think you've heard all my stories?

GLADYS: Because I've heard some 10 times! I could recount them in unison

26

right along with you.

JOE: There are lots of things I've never told you.

GLADYS: Okay. Tell me a story *(Long pause)* Well . . .

JOE: Give me a second. *(Pause)* Okay, here's one. Several years ago, I was working late in the press room, proofing the layout. I had a really quick deadline. Thirty minutes to go and the paper would run late.

GLADYS: You were looking over the paper, and you found a sports story in the obituaries, "McKinley wins in sudden death."

JOE: How did you know that?

GLADYS: You told me!

JOE: Are you sure?

GLADYS: Three times . . .

JOE: Fine. That's fine. Maybe we shouldn't talk. Maybe this marriage would be better if we just read each other's mind.

GLADYS: Let's just drop the subject.

JOE: If we drop the subject of not having anything to say, then what are we going to say? Maybe we should talk jibberish. At least there would be noise.

GLADYS: That's not the point I was . . .

JOE: Charades—that's the answer. We *talked* the first 25 years of our marriage. Let's try sign and smoke signals for the next 25.

(Joe stands up and begins to prompt her nonverbally to play Charades.)

GLADYS: Sit back down! This is embarrassing. What if one of the deacons walks in or the pastor? Sit down, you silly old man! You never give in, do you? *(Joe motions for her to guess.)* No, I'm not. *(She finally relents.)* Okay. *(Joe charades as the guess would suggest.)* Uh—five—-five words—first word—little word—the—is—in—of—a—that's it. *(Joe signals "on the nose.")* Second word—This is crazy. Stop this—Okay! Okay! You're thinking—you have a headache—uh—think—okay. Okay—concentrate. Okay, one syllable—dream—know! That's it? Oh, that's not it—knew? Okay! A new—right? *(Joe makes a book with his hands.)*

GLADYS: *(Gladys says to herself.)* Thank goodness, it's only five words. *(To Joe)* Henderson is laughing. *(To waiter)* Hey, Henderson, you have seen us here for over 25 years. Have you ever seen him act like this? You own this place now. Can't you kick him out? *(Back to the game)* Okay! You're opening your hands—you're uh—what *are* you doing? A book! Your hands are a book—Okay! Reading—you're singing—you're talking—you're telling a story—telling? Story! Story! *(To herself)* This is like something you see in a play. *(Again guessing)* A new story—fourth word—two syllables—two letters? Oh, just two! A new story to—a story to think? A new story to hear? A new story to tell! *(Joe gives the "on the nose" sign.)* Oh, I get it! Now I have a new story to tell. So does Henderson!

JOE: I thought you'd never come through.

GLADYS: I can't believe that a 50-year-old man would make such a fool of himself in a public place.

JOE: Don't tell the kids. I'd never live it down.

GLADYS: I guess we do have things to talk about. We've just spent 20 years raising the kids. Now they're on their own. The four of us are now the two of us.

JOE: Here's a story you haven't heard. I remember this like it was yesterday. I rushed you to the hospital when Angela was on her way. I was so excited. Jonathan didn't have a clue about what was happening. Your mother just picked him up and said, "Little John, your mommy's gonna bring you a little sister or brother." Isn't it strange how you remember little things like that? I remember the doctor as he approached me six hours later. He looked nervous. He said that there were some complications beyond the natural process of things. I just stood there—frozen. I didn't know what to ask. I didn't know what to say. That was the loneliest feeling I've ever had. I'd forgotten what life was like before you. I remembered those days in that small frame house on Gunter Road when we ate nothing but peas and cornbread. Those walks. I remembered at that moment how much I needed you. I prayed longer and stronger than I had ever prayed before. I said, "God, I don't have anything to give. I don't know what I'm supposed to say. But please—don't take Gladys—take *my* life, not hers. Take my life." Those were my words as I saw that door open to the labor room. Three hours had passed since the complications. The doctor walked out with a big smile on his face. He didn't really have to say anything. That smile said the one word I wanted to hear—a beautiful, magical word—*alive.*

(Black out)

GLADYS' VOICE ON TAPE: *(Singing a cappella)*

Great is thy faithfulness, O God my Father,
There is no shadow of turning with thee;
Thou changest not, thy compassions, they fail not;
As thou hast been thou forever wilt be.
Great is thy faithfulness!
Great is thy faithfulness!
Morning by morning new mercies I see;
All I have needed thy hand hath provided;
Great is thy faithfulness, Lord, unto me![1]

Scene Five

(Gladys and Joe entering)

GLADYS: I had a strange suspicion that this was the place we'd come tonight.

JOE: After 40 years of celebrating, it seemed only appropriate.

GLADYS: It's like an old friend.

JOE: *(Waving offstage)* Good evening, Henderson.

GLADYS: They stopped taking our order in the fifties.

JOE: Well, we kept orderin' the same dadblame thing. I guess they just yell back to the cook to get the spaghetti sauce warmed up.

(They sit.)

GLADYS: We're just about to the end of our road.

JOE: Oh, come on, Glad. Don't talk that way.

GLADYS: Well, we *are.* We've had a wonderful life; two of the best kids one could ask for; a nice home . . .

JOE: Small but nice.

GLADYS: What would you change?

28

JOE: What?

GLADYS: If you were 18 years old with your whole life before you, what would you change?

JOE: Oh, I don't think I'd change anything. *(Pause)* I think I'd try not to worry so much.

GLADYS: I think I'd hug the kids more often when they were small.

JOE: You practically smothered them as it was.

GLADYS: I think I'd make more of an attempt to teach you to dance.

JOE: That's why they say Methodist girls shouldn't marry Baptist boys. And nobody should marry a preacher's kid.

GLADYS: But strange as it was, you turned out okay.

JOE: Kids did too. Although I'm positive to this day that Jonathan has worms from kissing all those pets we brought in.

GLADYS: *We* brought in! We? *You* were the stray's best friend. I remember at one time we had a Labrador retriever, a poodle-looking dog, and a cocker spaniel all in our backyard.

JOE: Yeah, we had some of the strangest looking puppies that year.

GLADYS: Strange muts, muddy kids, good food, and lots of love. That would just about sum it all up.

JOE: I remember Angela asking me when she was five, "Are you the richest man in town?" I thought it was an awful strange question. She had to notice that our house was smaller than the houses downtown. I just said, "Sweetheart, I'm not the richest man in town, but I've got the richest heavenly Father in the world."

(Black out)

TAPED VOICES OF JOE AND GLADYS—

JOE: "What shall we then say to these things? If God be for us, who can be against us?" *(Rom. 8:31, KJV)*

GLADYS: "He that spared not his own Son, but delivered him up for us all" *(Rom. 8:32a, KJV)*.

JOE: "How shall he not with him also freely give us all things? *(Rom. 8:32b, KJV)*

GLADYS: "Who shall separate us from the love of Christ? Shall tribulation, or distress, or persecution, or famine, or nakedness, or peril, or sword? Nay, in all these things we are more than conquerors through him that loved us. For I am persuaded, that neither death, nor life, nor angels, nor principalities, nor powers, nor things present, nor things to come, nor height, nor depth, nor any other creature, shall be able to separate us from the love of God, which is in Christ Jesus our Lord" *(Rom. 8:35,37-39, KJV)*.

Scene Six

(As lights come up, Joe is sitting by himself at the table. He is talking to Henderson.)

JOE: The meal was excellent—really. Now if you trust me, the oldest and most faithful patron of the Riverfront, allow me to lock up. *(Pause—listening to the response)* Now, Henderson, I've seen you lock up a hundred times. I'll just latch the back door and mash in the button on the front entrance. *(Pause)* No—go ahead and turn out the lights. I'll use the candles. A candle is not worth much unless you put it to good use. *(Pause)* Okay, you have a good night, too. *(Lights go off as Joe lights the two candles.)* Well, Lord, it's been three months since Gladys left to sing in Your choir. She has a beautiful voice, doesn't she? I miss it. I want to thank You for a wonderful wife. I could never figure why she married an old paper boy like me anyway. I thank You for her tender voice, her laughter, even the aggravating gift she had of reading my mind. She was always listening, always hopeful, always faithful. I always thought I'd be the one leaving *her* here, but she slipped away. I know she's a happy woman now, because she's with the One she loves most. And all because You first loved us. Thank You, Father.

(Joe sings.)

Great is thy faithfulness! Great is thy faithfulness!

Morning by morning new mercies I see;

All I have needed thy hand hath provided;

Great is thy faithfulness, Lord, unto me![2]

(Joe blows out the candle.)

---

[1]Thomas O. Chisholm, "Great Is Thy Faithfulness." Copyright © 1923. Renewal 1951 by Hope Publishing Co., Carol Stream, IL 60188. All rights reserved. Used by permission.
[2]Ibid.

The Prisoners
by John Lee Welton

(Church service, discussion)

Thought: "How would Peter and Judas respond to each other's denial of Christ."

Characters: 3 males or 2 males, 1 female

Props: Small table, two chairs, pitcher, two glasses, basket of bread.

Setting: A space. A man is seen setting two chairs on the stage, Right Center and Left Center. He moves to a table Down Center which contains two glasses, a pitcher and a small basket of bread. He checks to see that everything is in order. The 1st Man steps in looking around tentatively.

ATTENDANT: Come in. *(The 1st Man hesitates and backs up a step.)* It's all right. Come on in. *(1st Man moves into the room, looking about nervously. He crosses the room until his back is to the Attendant.)* Won't you . . .

1st MAN: *(Jerks around, frightened.)* Wha . . . ?

ATTENDANT: Won't you sit down? Take that chair.

1st MAN: *(Moves to chair, but doesn't sit. He simply runs his hands over the chair, exploring it almost in wonderment.)* I'd—I'd almost forgotten what a chair looked like. *(He looks about again, then speaks suspiciously to the Attendant.)* What is this place? Why did you bring me here?

ATTENDANT: You came because you wanted to.

1st MAN: I—I can't seem to remember anything before I walked through that door.

ATTENDANT: As to where you are, call it a resting place—a point in time. Won't you sit down?

1st MAN: But I'm not tired. I don't need rest. *(Looking at his hands in a puzzled way)* As a matter of fact, it's like I'm numb. I can barely feel my body. *(Turning to the Attendant)* What's going on here? Why won't you tell me where I am?

ATTENDANT: Call it a place of the

30

mind, if you want to.

1st MAN: Blast it! Can't you give me a straight answer when I ask you a question? *Where am I?*

ATTENDANT: You're where you want to be—where you asked to be.

1st MAN: I don't know what kind of game you're playing, but *I did not ask to come here. (A bit off balance)* At—at least I don't think I did. Look, am I a prisoner or something? I—I really don't remember where I was or how I got here.

ATTENDANT: You will, in time. Won't you sit down? *(1st Man stands staring stubbornly at the Attendant, then suddenly, almost defiantly, sits. A second man appears. The Attendant turns and sees him.)* Ah, here you are. Come in.

2nd MAN: Where am I? I . . .

1st MAN: *(Sarcastically)* Don't bother to ask. You won't get a straight answer. *(To the Attendant)* Is he another prisoner?

ATTENDANT: No. You're both free to do as you will. *(To 2nd Man)* Won't you sit down?

1st MAN: You might as well sit. He won't give up on you till you do.

2nd MAN: Thank you.

ATTENDANT: *(Starting toward exit)* Please refresh yourselves. *(Indicating table)* There's something to eat and drink if you wish. I'll be nearby if you need me. Just call.

(He exits. The men look at each other curiously for a moment, then the 2nd Man clears his throat, crosses to the table, pours from the pitcher and starts to drink.)

1st MAN: I wouldn't drink that if I were you.

2nd MAN: *(Lowering the goblet)* Why not?

1st MAN: Could be poisoned—or drugged. Maybe that's it. They've kept us drugged. Something crazy's going on here. I don't remember where I've been or how I got here—and apparently you're not much better off.

2nd MAN: You're right. I *don't* recall where I've been.

1st MAN: *(Looking at him curiously)* Have we met before? You look familiar.

2nd MAN: I really don't know. Everything's so foggy in my head, I can't seem to even remember my name.

1st MAN: It's Peter.

2nd MAN: What did you say?

1st MAN: Peter. That's your name. I just remembered. I don't know why I remembered, but I *do* know you from someplace—someplace a long time ago.

2nd MAN: *(Slowly tasting the name)* Peter. Yes—yes, that's right. You say you knew me? Where?

1st MAN: I don't know. I don't remember that. Just that it was a long time ago—and yet it's like only an instant since then. Do—do you recall ever knowing me? My own name seems to be hiding somewhere at the back of my brain, almost as if it's afraid to come out.

2nd MAN: *(Looking at him closely)* I—I do seem to remember you from somewhere. Yes, it's slowly coming back to me now. We—we traveled together and worked together for some reason. Judas, it had something to do with someone we both loved.

1st MAN: What did you call me?

2nd MAN: I—I think I called you "Judas." Would that have been your name?

1st MAN: I—I don't know that name. I . . . *(He turns away, obviously trying to painfully connect the name with something.)* Yes, I do. It seems—somewhere—a long time ago I was called by that. *(Turning suddenly and sitting)* No! I don't want to remember. It's all wrong. *(Suddenly moving toward the exit)* I want to go back where I came from—wherever it was. *(Calling off)* Hey, you out there. Take me out of here—*NOW!*

2nd MAN: Jesus. That's who we both loved.

1st MAN: NO! I don't want to hear it all again! *(Covering his ears)*

2nd MAN: *(Excitedly)* It was Jesus that brought us together. It's all coming back, now! The wonders and the miracles—it's all flooding back as if it were happening right now. How we walked with Him and laughed with Him. How He shared His food with us and taught us, and how you . . . *(He suddenly stops and looks at Judas.)*

1st MAN: *(Straightening up—he speaks in an almost lifeless tone.)* So . . . the echo never stops. It goes on and on for eternity.

2nd MAN: *(Shaking his head in disbelief)* How could you do that? How could you kill Him?

1st MAN: *(Shouting at him) Don't say that!* I didn't kill Him! The Sanhedrin, the Romans, that stupid mob—they killed Him—not me. He could have stopped them, but He didn't—He killed Himself. It wasn't me!

2nd MAN: I remember it clearly now. It *was* you.

1st MAN: NO! Don't you see? I loved Him. I wanted Him to be *king.* I did ev-

erything I could to make Him king. Nobody seemed to understand that. You all made snide remarks about how tightly I held the money bags, but without my managing, you would have all gone hungry. And how could we have cared for the poor? I made money for Him so He could do His work.

2nd MAN: You sold Him for 30 pieces of silver.

1st MAN: No! It wasn't the money! God knows it wasn't the money! I flung it back in their faces. What was 30 pieces of silver? Nothing—trash! When He was king 30 pieces of silver would be *nothing.* All I wanted was to make Him king!

2nd MAN: Your way, Judas. Your way—not His!

1st MAN: While He was fussing over the petty troubles of that rabble trailing at His heels, He was letting His kingdom slip by. Don't you see? All I wanted to do was to give Him a push—force Him into action—make Him do what I knew He must do. Make Him see what I saw—the opportunity to set us all free from the tyranny of the Romans.

2nd MAN: But you betrayed Him!

1st MAN: *I did not mean to betray Him!* Don't you understand? I thought He would call on the power of God to protect Him. We had seen so many miracles. I thought the least He could do would be to protect Himself. He tricked me! If He was determined to die, He used me as a tool. If God had destined Jesus to die, then He destined me to help Him do it. Why should I be blamed throughout eternity for doing what God had destined me to do?

2nd MAN: Don't blame God! He may

have allowed the opportunity to be there, but it was your decision to betray Jesus. You're guilty, not God!

1st MAN: Guilt? And who are you to talk about guilt? "On this rock," Jesus said. Your faith was to be the rock He would build His church on. Some rock! When He was arrested, you denied even knowing Him! The rock crumbled! You turned your face away from Him as if He never existed. At least I had the guts to stand up and say I knew Him when I threw the silver trash back in their faces. I at least admitted the pain of what I did when I hanged myself in shame. And what did you do? You denied Him—not once, but three times. And you have the gall to call *me* guilty!

(The 2nd Man backs up slowly, then turns and sits in the nearest chair. There is a long silence while the 1st Man turns away, wrapped up in his own anger. The 2nd Man finally speaks in a low tone.)

2nd MAN: You're right. I have no call to judge you. Since that morning, I've carried the burden of that cowardice with me, but I shoved it into the back of my mind. All my life I tried to play the strong man, the rock, the tower of strength doing the Master's work. And yet, that one night's cowardice has chipped away at me, sapping my strength, making me less than I could have been. By hiding it away in the darkest corner of my soul, I'm still denying Jesus. God help me, I'm no better than you!

1st MAN: I—I'm sorry. That was very cruel of me to do that. I've carried the sharp-edged knife of my sin for so long, I find it easy to hack away at the soft spots of others.

2nd MAN: I was so afraid that night. When I saw Him beaten and bleeding, I doubted. Maybe—maybe it was all a hoax; maybe Jesus had fooled us like some clever magician. I doubted that anyone so weak and pitiful as He looked could be the Son of God. And I was afraid, afraid that I had risked my life for a failure, a madman who had spread His madness to us, made me a part of His mad world. I saw His bleeding body and I was afraid of the pain that might be mine if I said I knew Him. I saw His Kingdom tumbling down around us all, taking us with it to the cross. And so—I said I didn't know Him, had never known Him. I denied Him and I'm no better for my weakness than you are for your sin. Forgive me for accusing you, Judas. I had no right to judge you.

1st MAN: Did He trick us all and make fools of us? Have I suffered all this for nothing?

2nd MAN: No. Whatever fools we've been, it was not a trick. When He died on the cross, the miracles didn't stop. He came back to us.

1st MAN: I don't understand.

2nd MAN: He came back from the dead. We talked with Him again, ate with Him, and the miracles still happened. Marvelous powers were given to us to do His work. Since that time, His teachings grew and spread across the lands till His name came to mean life itself, everlasting life! He became King in a different way than we all thought. He became King of eternity!

1st MAN: King of eternity. And I tried to bend His will to mine. Make Him the king I wanted Him to be. He really came back?

2nd MAN: Yes.

1st MAN: I wish I could have been there and talked to Him again. I wish I could kneel at His feet and ask forgiveness for the pain I caused Him. I did love Him, Peter. Whatever else history may say about me, I did love Him. I so wanted Him to be king, and I wanted to know I had a part in making Him king. I tried to force Him to my will, to make Him fit my mold, my ideas. I guess He tried to tell me, to make me understand what His Kingdom was all about, but I wouldn't listen. I thought I knew what it should be, and I went about my business pushing and shoving and trying to make it happen my way. If only I had listened to Him, maybe I would have understood. I wish I could tell Him I'm sorry.

2nd MAN: So do I. In all the time I was with Him after He came back from the tomb, I never asked Him to forgive me for denying Him. There were so many times my heart cried out to tell Him and ask His forgiveness, but the same cowardice that made me deny Him imprisoned the words inside me.

1st MAN: How could you be with Him and not say anything? My heart would have screamed out for Him to forgive me. Oh, if only He could have heard my words! To be with Him and not say anything! If only I'd had that chance.

2nd MAN: *Don't!* Don't accuse me with that. The pain is great enough with my own accusation.

1st MAN: I'm sorry. I didn't mean it as an accusation for you. It—it was just a lost wish for myself.

(The Attendant has appeared at the entrance and has been listening to the last few words. The men do not see him until he speaks.)

ATTENDANT: Not lost, Judas. Not lost at all.

1st MAN: You—you've been listening to everything we said?

ATTENDANT: Yes, but I knew it all before you said it. I've known it all from the beginning.

2nd MAN: Who are you?

ATTENDANT: One who loves you very much. Please, come and refresh yourselves with me. *(He goes to the table and pours from the pitcher. The men move to each side of the table. The 2nd Man seems to recognize the face of the Attendant.)*

2nd MAN: Master—is it You?

ATTENDANT: Yes, Peter.

1st MAN: But—but we thought You were just a servant of some sort! Forgive us! *(He sinks to his knees.)*

ATTENDANT: No, Judas. *(Attendant kneels and helps the 1st Man to his feet.)* You were forgiven long ago, when your heart cried out for forgiveness. You had only but to ask. Here, eat and drink.

(The Attendant hands each man a glass, then reaches down and breaks the bread. He hands each of them one half the loaf. As the bread reaches their mouths they all freeze in tableau. As the lights fade, the Attendant focuses on the 1st Man and smiles gently at him.)

Production Notes: *If the director feels uncomfortable using an actor to portray Jesus, an alternate ending may be used. Simply change the 2nd Man's line from "Master—is it You?" to "Are you sent*

The Temptation of Joseph
by Gerald Morris

Characters: 2 males, 1 female
Props: A bench for Satan, a blanket for Mary to hold as the baby.
Costumes: Plain, modern work clothes—Satan's darker.

(Mary sits alone in the stable on the floor with her baby in her arms. Satan sits on the other side of the stage on a bench. Mary is singing softly. Joseph enters, carrying a lantern. Note: All props unless otherwise indicated are pantomimed.)

MARY: Oh, there you are.

JOSEPH: *(Wearily)* No luck.

MARY: None?

JOSEPH: No. There won't be a room in the whole country until the census is finished. We'll be in the stable for several more days.

MARY: We'll get by.

JOSEPH: How's the baby?

MARY: Look for yourself. *(He does, tentatively.)* Oh Joseph, you can get closer than that. He's just a baby. He won't hurt you.

JOSEPH: He looks awfully red.

MARY: All babies look awfully red.

JOSEPH: Oh, then He's all right?

MARY: Of course. Hang up the lantern somewhere. I don't want it to shine in His eyes and wake Him up.

JOSEPH: Where?

MARY: I don't know; find a rafter somewhere.

JOSEPH: Here's a hook.

MARY: Oh Joseph, not there. It puts the baby in that shadow of those beams.

JOSEPH: I thought that was what you wanted.

MARY: Well, I want to be able to see Him.

JOSEPH: *(A bit snappishly)* Well, it's the only place.

MARY: It can't be the only place. This is a stable.

JOSEPH: Well, find a place yourself then! *(He pauses.)* I'm sorry, Mary. I'm just irritable, I guess.

MARY: I know. You've been up all night. You leave the lantern there. Look, you can still see Jesus in the shadow. He almost gives off His own light.

SATAN: *(Mocking)* He almost gives off His own light. *(Joseph whirls around to face him.)*

MARY: You see, Joseph? Joseph, you're not looking.

JOSEPH: *(Glancing back at her)* I see, I see.

SATAN: She sees a little light surrounding the precious little boy. Look, Joseph, look! Don't you see it, Joseph?

JOSEPH: *(Quietly)* No, I don't.

SATAN: What do you see, Joseph?

JOSEPH: I see darkness. This whole stable is dark. It's like a hole in the ground.

SATAN: A grave, perhaps?

JOSEPH: I don't know. It's just dark.

SATAN: But there's light from the lantern. And the moon is shining right in the window. Maybe it's all in your mind, little man. If your mind is dark, how can you see light? *(Pause)* Look at how the shadow falls on the baby. He's right at the intersection of those two beams. He's

35

in the middle of a cross.

JOSEPH: In the shadow of a cross.

SATAN: Not a good beginning for a baby, is it?

JOSEPH: Leave me alone, will you?

SATAN: Irritable, aren't we?

JOSEPH: Just go away!

SATAN: I can't leave you, Joseph. You're stuck with me. *(Pause)* It's not easy being a father when you know you aren't really the father, is it?

JOSEPH: Shut up!

SATAN: I wonder if she's telling the truth? Conceived by an angel, she says.

JOSEPH: You lie! She's telling the truth!

SATAN: Surely you've wondered.

JOSEPH: Never.

SATAN: You can't lie to me, little man. If you had never wondered, I couldn't have suggested it. *(Pause)* Not that it makes any difference, of course. Whether the father was an angel or a human, it's still not you, is it?

JOSEPH: So what?

SATAN: Oh, I'm just curious. How does it feel to be a proxy father for God—assuming that God's really the Father?

JOSEPH: Shut up!

SATAN: A guardian, of sorts. Oh well, I suppose someone has to take care of God's mistakes. . . .

JOSEPH: *(After a long pause)* "You shall love the Lord your God with all your heart and with all your soul and with all your might" *(Deut. 6:5, NASB).*

MARY: Joseph, what are you doing over there?

JOSEPH: I . . . I didn't want to disturb you and the baby.

MARY: Oh Joseph, come closer. You

seem so frightened of Him sometimes. I guess that's because you're a man. You're so helpless with children.

SATAN: Helpless.

JOSEPH: I'm not afraid of Him. I'm just not gentle like you.

SATAN: How does it feel to be helpless?

JOSEPH: I don't know what you're talking about.

MARY: I just mean that you never . . .

JOSEPH: No, not you.

MARY: What? *(She stares at him, confused and worried.)*

SATAN: You're being used, Joseph.

JOSEPH: Used?

SATAN: Did God *ask* you if you would play daddy for Him? It looks like you were drafted.

JOSEPH: If I *had* been asked, I would have done it.

SATAN: If you had been asked . . . ? Joseph, with logic like that you should have been a Pharisee. The point is that God didn't ask you.

JOSEPH: He didn't, did He?

SATAN: I should have had it this easy in the garden. At least in the garden they had a choice. Nobody made them do anything. You! You were pulled out of the ranks and stuck with a job that no one else would do. You're a patsy, Joseph.

JOSEPH: Then I have no choice?

SATAN: What a genius. How are you to worship your God now? And what kind of worship is it if it's forced?

JOSEPH: *(Slowly)* I can choose to obey. Yes, I can choose to . . .

SATAN: You're not listening, stupid! You can't choose at all! All you can do is be chosen. What an honor! You get to be a slave.

JOSEPH: *(More firmly)* At least I'll be a slave of the Lord.

SATAN: You're a fool, carpenter.

JOSEPH: So be it.

(In the next speeches, Joseph is drawn between Satan and Mary. The lines grow gradually louder.)

MARY: Joseph, look at Him. He's playing with my finger.

JOSEPH: I see.

SATAN: Joseph, look at Him. He's sleeping in the shadow of a cross.

JOSEPH: I see that too.

MARY: He's so strong. He'll be good help in the shop.

SATAN: At least until He dies.

MARY: He's such a healthy boy.

SATAN: Too bad He'll be dead so young.

MARY: Oh, He does have a strong grasp.

SATAN: See His hands? Now imagine them with nails in them.

JOSEPH: *(Shouting)* What do you want with me? *(Mary looks up, confused.)*

SATAN: I want you to understand what you're getting yourself into. You're playing foster father for a dead child. He's doomed, Joseph!

JOSEPH: Get out of here!

MARY: Joseph, what's wrong?

SATAN: Joseph, what's wrong? You said you saw darkness around the child. Well, you were right. You saw doom. He'll live in sorrow all His life, and you will share it with Him. That's what following God is!

JOSEPH: Stop it! I don't want to hear any more!

MARY: Joseph, please! Why don't you lie down and get some rest? You've been up all night. Joseph, it's almost morning.

SATAN: It's almost morning. You must be *dead* tired.

JOSEPH: *(With strength)* Quiet!

MARY: Joseph! The baby! *(She returns to the baby and, to comfort it, begins humming a tune.)*

SATAN: *(Spitefully)* He should have been stillborn.

JOSEPH: But He wasn't, and the night was torn apart.

SATAN: You're a fool, little man. You'll live in sorrow, don't you see?

JOSEPH: If I have to. *(Joseph walks up to the baby.)* Sleep in peace, little One. You have come to do great things.

MARY: Now can you get some rest, Joseph? The sun is rising.

JOSEPH: *(Without looking)* I know.

(Lights out.)

Lazarus
by Gerald Morris

Cast: Lazarus; Mary, his sister; Jesus.
Setting: A bench.

Note: *The Christ in this play is far from serene. In a week He will be crucified and, knowing that, He is worried. He is frustrated by Lazarus' attitude. He should be played with all of this in mind. A serene Christ in this play will cripple its effectiveness.*

(Lazarus sits alone. Mary, his sister, enters.)

MARY: *(Entering)* Lazarus, there you are. What's wrong?

LAZARUS: Nothing. Nothing.

MARY: Nothing? Then why are you sitting out here?

LAZARUS: I'm thinking.

MARY: Come inside to the party, Lazarus. It's *your* party, after all. Yesterday you were dead, and today you are alive. Come have something to drink.

LAZARUS: Yesterday I was alive; today I am dead again.

MARY: What?

LAZARUS: Nothing. I'm sorry.

MARY: Then come inside.

LAZARUS: *(Sharply)* In a minute! I'm thinking.

MARY: *(Sitting next to him)* What are you thinking about.

LAZARUS: I can't explain it to you, Mary.

MARY: Why not?

LAZARUS: You wouldn't understand.

MARY: Is it about Him?

LAZARUS: Who?

MARY: Who? Jesus, who else?

LAZARUS: Yes, I suppose. In a way.

MARY: Isn't He wonderful?

LAZARUS: Wonderful? No, Mary. He's far beyond wonderful. I'm not sure what He is, but He has . . . He has power over things that . . .

MARY: You don't know how to thank Him, is that it?

LAZARUS: Well . . .

MARY: Oh Lazarus, you can just tell Him thank you, and He'll understand. Trust Him.

LAZARUS: There's more to it than that.

MARY: *(Pulling him toward the door)* Oh, don't be shy. Come inside and thank Him now. He's just inside the door.

LAZARUS: *(Pulling away)* In a minute! *(Pauses, helplessly)* I'm thinking. *(Jesus appears at the door and watches.)*

MARY: Well hurry. He's about to start teaching, and you don't want to miss that.

LAZARUS: I told you. In a minute.

JESUS: *(Stepping forward)* Lazarus, I brought you a drink.

MARY: Oh Master! You shouldn't do things like that. Here, let me get that.

JESUS: Be still, Mary.

MARY: Lazarus, here He is now. He was just coming to thank You, Master.

JESUS: I don't think so.

MARY: Oh yes, he was. Weren't you, Lazarus?

LAZARUS: I don't know, Mary.

MARY: Don't know? Oh Lazarus, He made you live again.

LAZARUS: I know.

JESUS: I'm sorry, Lazarus.

MARY: Sorry?

JESUS: It had to be. Before God made the earth, He knew you, and you were chosen to see Him and then leave Him.

LAZARUS: I have seen true life. Now I have to return to death again. Why?

MARY: You're going to die again? Oh Master, can't You get him out of it?

LAZARUS: Be quiet, Mary! I *am* dead, don't you see? Before He called me from the tomb I was alive. I was with . . . *(He pauses, groping for words. Finally he gives up.)* And there is where life is. This *is* death, Mary, nor am I out of it.

MARY: I don't understand.

LAZARUS: I told you so.

JESUS: I didn't want to call you back any more than you wanted to be called back, Lazarus.

LAZARUS: Then why? Jesus, do You know what was the first thing I saw when they unwrapped my face? I saw the

38

face of my neighbor, Saul. He was trying to pretend to be happy that I was alive, but I could see how disappointed he really was. He owes me money. Right now, he's inside there shouting and drinking and pretending and maybe even believing that he is happy. Is that what You called me back to?

You know what I saw then? I saw the doctor who hadn't been able to cure me trying to explain to everyone why You had been able to help me when he couldn't. Did You see the way he looked at You?

JESUS: I saw.

LAZARUS: He hates You, Master, because You did what he could not. Am I to be happy to return to jealousy and hatred?

You know what I saw just a few minutes ago, before I came out here? I saw a harlot entice one of the celebrators away from my party. At this moment they are making love somewhere—for money. Love for money! I'm supposed to be pleased to come back to a place where people buy and sell love?

JESUS: I know, Lazarus.

LAZARUS: It's too hard, Master. It would have been better never to have seen the glory of God than to see Him and then have to leave it.

JESUS: *(Suddenly angry)* Would it? Would it really? I don't think so, Lazarus.

LAZARUS: What could be worse than to be here and know how much better it is there?

JESUS: To be here and not know that there is anything better, anywhere. Lazarus! You have seen the Creator of the universe. How can you hate His creatures? You have seen the joy of His light. How dare you stay out here in the darkness. How dare you keep that joy to yourself.

MARY: What joy? What is it, Lazarus?

JESUS: Tell her about it.

LAZARUS: *(Slowly, seeking words)* I saw . . . Mary, I saw the Lord—He was . . . He was . . . Jesus, I can't! How can I describe it? No one will understand. Not unless they see it.

JESUS: Now you're catching on! They've got to see the Lord themselves. Help them.

LAZARUS: Why me?

JESUS: *(Exasperated)* Why you? You have seen God! Lazarus, what do you think *I'm* doing here?

LAZARUS: You came . . . here . . .

JESUS: From God.

LAZARUS: Why *did* You come?

JESUS: Let me tell you a story, Lazarus. Once there was a young girl, much like your sister Mary here. In fact, her name was Mary too. She was a virgin, betrothed to marry a carpenter of Nazareth named Joseph. Before she was married, though, she was visited by an angel.

MARY: Oh, I love Your parables.

JESUS: This isn't a parable, Mary. This one is true.

LAZARUS: Master, do I have to listen to a story?

JESUS: Listen to this one. The young girl and her betrothed were visited by angels who told them that the girl was to bear a son. But she was a virgin.

LAZARUS: You said this was a true story.

JESUS: And you don't believe in miracles? You? (Lazarus looks down, ashamed.) The two were married. Then Joseph had to go to Bethlehem for Augustus' census. While they were there, Mary had a child.

LAZARUS: Master, what does this mean? It's a nice story and everything, but . . .

JESUS: "And there were shepherds living out in the fields nearby, keeping watch over their flocks by night. An angel of the Lord appeared to them, and the glory of the Lord shone around them, and they were terrified. But the angel said to them, 'Do not be afraid. I bring you good news of great joy that will be for all the people. Today in the town of David a Savior has been born to you; he is Christ the Lord' " (Luke 1:8-11, NIV).

LAZARUS: You mean the baby of Mary and Joseph . . .

JESUS: Was God Himself. The Christ. The Messiah.

(There is a long pause. Mary and Lazarus stare at Jesus. Then Mary understands. She walks slowly toward Him, but before she reaches Him she is overcome with awe. She sinks to her knees. Lazarus crosses to her and puts his hand on her shoulder.)

MARY: And it's You. Jesus, He is You, isn't He?

JESUS: And Mary knelt in the stable where they lived and Joseph stood above her, and they held under their human protection the God who made them. God came to earth, Lazarus.

(Lazarus drops to his knees next to Mary.)

MARY: Our Father we praise You, for You have sent Your Son to come to earth.

LAZARUS: I think I understand.

MARY: He is God, isn't He? Isn't He, Lazarus?

LAZARUS: He's showing me the way.

MARY: (Rising) Jesus is God!

LAZARUS: He came from the presence of God the Father to see us and to let us see Him . . .

MARY: He is the Father, and the Father is Him.

LAZARUS: And . . . in the same way, we who have seen God, who have known His glory must go out to the world . . .

MARY: Jesus . . .

LAZARUS: . . . to show them what we have seen!

MARY: . . . is God!

LAZARUS: And the motive . . .

MARY: Messiah!

LAZARUS: . . . is love!

MARY: The Messiah has come to earth!

LAZARUS: And we too should go to the earth.

MARY: We have seen God!

LAZARUS: That they too may see God!

MARY and LAZARUS: God has come to earth!

JESUS: "Suddenly a great company of the heavenly host appeared with the angel, praising God and saying, 'Glory to God in the highest, and on earth peace on whom his favor rests' " (Luke 2:13-14, NIV).

LAZARUS: (Quietly) What am I doing out here?

MARY: Let's go inside, Lazarus. (They exit.)

JESUS: (Still kneeling) Amen.

(Lights out)

Writer's Note: *The other major religious celebration in our churches is Easter, and both of the two years that I worked with a drama group we did Easter productions. The first year it was not a play but rather a series of three monologues, all set in or around the home of Mary, the mother of John Mark. All we really know about the home of Mary is that it was often used as a meeting place by Jewish Christians after the Resurrection. I have taken this information and, for the purpose of the drama, made several assumptions: (1) that it was in this house that Christ and His disciples shared the Last Supper, (2) that Mary's son Mark was the "certain young man" who followed Christ to Gethsemane (Mark 14:51-52), and (3) that the disciples had gathered again in Mary's upper room when Thomas met the resurrected Christ. None of these assumptions can be substantiated with anything resembling proof, but on the other hand none is completely illogical either, and they do certainly help the drama.*

DRAMATIC AND COMEDY MESSAGE SKETCHES

Christians on Strike
by Bill Taylor

(Worship Service, Discussion)

Cast: Reporter (R), Striking Christian (SC), Non-Union Replacement Disciple (N.U.R.D.)

R: *(Enters with microphone in hand.)* In a somewhat strange set of events all of the Christians across our country have walked out of their churches and have declared themselves "on strike." Many are forming picket lines and protesting a number of arguments. With me right now is Charlie Smurk, a striking Christian. Mr. Smurk, why are you on strike?

SC: Well, Mr. Lather, we're just fed up with our benefits. You know, as children of the King we shouldn't have to continue living among these heathen, shopping with them, going to bars around them. I mean, with this AIDS epidemic going around—that's the last straw! Well, who wants a disease that you can't avoid?

R: Okay, so the benefits is one issue. Is there anything else that's ruffling the feathers of you Christians?

SC: You bet, Dan! We're tired of this FREE-GRACE AGENCY deal. I mean, why did Management set this up in the first place? What logic is it to just *give away* eternal life JUST for the asking without working for it! Of course,

we've gone along with it for some time now, but for 20 years I've worked hard in my church, paid my tithe, and attended church . . . and then, one day, some knucklehead who's like the armpit of the human race comes in and gets the same benefit package as the rest of us veterans. We've established a good team, here, to have it taken over by morons who don't deserve it!

R: Well, thank you, Mr. Smurk. Seems that there are *two* main issues on the line with these Striking Christians . . . first, the *benefits* of living conditions among the heathen, I mean, non-Christians, and secondly, the free-grace agency now imposed by the Owner. Oddly enough, ever since the Union Christians have gone on strike, the Owner has replaced His veterans with Non-Union Replacement Disciples or N.U.R.D.S. *(chuckle)*. With me is a N.U.R.D., Mr. I.B. Free. Mr. Free, are you concerned about harassment from these Union Christians?

N.U.R.D.: Well, Mr. Lather, I can only speak for myself, but ever since the Owner called I'm not concerned about anything else but working for Him.

R: Well, you understand the issues the Striking Christians are protesting. We know that after talking with the Owner, He is not willing to change one dotted "i" or one crossed "t" in the contract.

Do you have any problems with that package deal?

N.U.R.D.: Absolutely not, Dan. You see if it wasn't for the benefits I couldn't have become a N.U.R.D. in the first place. After what my Owner did for me and then considering me a person of worth to be on His team, it's just the greatest thing to ever happen to me. You know, many are called, but few are chosen.

R: Mr. Free, the Union Christians are calling you guys SCABS. Uh, how do you feel about being called such an ugly term?

N.U.R.D.: Dan, I know they mean it to put down, and really, they're not to blame, but I look at it this way . . . when there's a cut on the skin, a scab forms to protect that injury while healing is taking place. I know it's not pretty and appealing, but without the scab, infection, disease, and even death can take place. I really count it an honor to be called a scab for my Owner.

R: Mr. Free, what's your first assignment now that you've been called onto the team by the Owner?

N.U.R.D.: Well, Dan, there's so much to be done in such a short time. First, we're just going to focus on spreading the good news and getting more replacements. It's a job that the Union Christians didn't take too seriously. So we want to really do our best for the Owner.

R: What will you do if some Striking Christians start crossing the picket lines and rejoining the team?

N.U.R.D.: Well, Dan, that would be just super. The Owner has always said that whoever calls upon His name will be saved on the team. So I'm really looking for many to rethink their protests and get back to business working for the Owner.

R: How *does* the Owner feel about the Union Christians walking out on Him?

N.U.R.D.: Well, Dan, He's real hurt . . . but He's also real patient, too. He knows that most players indicated a zeal for the team early in their career, and He's counting on them to return to their first love. However, He also knows that the choice is theirs to receive or just reject His offer.

R: Any closing comments you'd like to offer to our TV viewers who are still undecided as to who to support in this strike?

N.U.R.D.: Dan, the Owner makes it clear to all who are weighing this strike . . . "choose you this day whom you will serve, whether it be God or man. As for me and my house, we will serve the Lord" *(Josh. 24:15, RSV, paraphrased).*

R: Thank you, Mr. Free and Mr. Smurk for joining us. I'm sure everyone will be following this strike very closely. Now back to you, Ted.

Being a Christian Servant
by Tom Eggleston

(Based on Matt. 25:31-46.)

(Worship service, Bible study)

Characters: 7

Note: *Each interrupter stands where they are in the congregation to speak. When the leader continues, each interrupter may be seated. The element of surprise makes this most effective, especially with the first interrupter.*

LEADER: *(At the podium)* In the Book of Matthew we find a discussion about the final judgment and what being a Christian servant means. Listen reverently to these words from Matthew 25. "When the Son of Man comes as King and all the angels with him, he will sit on his royal throne, and the people of all the nations will be gathered before him. Then he will divide them into two groups, just as a shepherd separates the sheep from the goats. He will put the righteous people at his right and the others at his left. Then the King will say to the people on his right, " 'Come, you that are blessed by my Father! Come and possess the kingdom which has been prepared for you ever since the creation of the world. I was hungry and you fed me, I was . . . ' " *(Matt. 25:31-35, GNB)*

INTERRUPTER #1: *(With intensity)* Wait just a minute, you didn't feed me. I was hungry and on the streets of _____. And I saw you drive right by me on your way to a fancy restaurant. You didn't even stop. No, you didn't feed me.

LEADER: Excuse me, sir, but you are interrupting the reading of this Scripture. Please sit down and let me continue. " '[I was] thirsty and you gave me a drink' " *(Matt. 25:35b, GNB)*.

INTERRUPTER #2: Hey, you didn't give me a drink. In fact, you just ignored me on that hot day in June. My car had broken down on the interstate and you just whizzed on by.

LEADER: I'm sorry, but we don't have time for this. Verse 35, " 'I was a stranger and you received me in your homes . . . ' " *(GNB)*

INTERRUPTER #3: Boy that's a joke. I came to visit your church and you were too busy visiting with your own little group. You didn't even take the time to say hello much less invite me to your home.

LEADER: Don't you have any reverence for the Word of God? Please allow me to continue, " '[I was] naked and you clothed me' " *(Matt. 25:36, GNB)*.

INTERRUPTER #4: I wish you could know how embarrassing it is to wear the same clothes day after day after day. After a while, it begins to wear down your dignity. I just wish you could know what it feels like.

LEADER: I'm sorry but these people don't want to hear about your problems. They've got problems of their own. Besides they came to listen to this Scripture. Verse 36 says, " 'I was sick and you took care of me . . . ' " *(GNB)*

INTERRUPTER #5: I'm afraid you didn't take care of me. I was put in a nursing home and the only times you came to visit me were on Christmas and Easter. Where were you the rest of the year?

LEADER: I'm afraid these interruptions are taking away from the Scripture. Please listen. " '[I was] in prison and you visited me' " *(Matt. 25:36, GNB)*.

INTERRUPTER #6: Prison is a lonely place. I ought to know, I was there for a year and felt like a number. I don't think anybody cared about what happened to me in there.

LEADER: " 'The righteous will then answer him,' ' "When, Lord, did we ever see you hungry and feed you, or thirsty and give you a drink? When did we ever see you a stranger and welcome you in our homes, or naked and clothe you? When did we ever see you sick or in prison, and visit you?" ' 'The King will reply,' ' "I tell you, whenever you did this for one of the least important of these brothers of mine, you did it for me!" ' 'Then he will say to those on his left,' ' "Away from me, you that are under God's curse! Away to the eternal fire which has been prepared for the Devil and his angels! I was hungry but you would not feed me . . . ' " *(Matt. 25:37-42a, GNB)*

INTERRUPTER #1: Yeah, that's right. I just needed a good hot meal. *(Stands and remains standing until the end.)*

LEADER: " . . . thirsty but you would not give me a drink" *(Matt. 25:42b, GNB).*

INTERRUPTER #2: All I needed was a helping hand and a cool drink of water. *(Stands and remains standing.)*

LEADER: "I was a stranger but you would not welcome me in your homes . . ." *(Matt. 25:43a, GNB)*

INTERRUPTER #3: Just a simple hello would have been a start. *(Stands)*

LEADER: " . . . naked but you would not clothe me" *(Matt. 25:43b, GNB).*

INTERRUPTER #4: All I needed was a clean dress and a little respect. *(Stands)*

LEADER: "I was sick . . . "

INTERRUPTER #5: I just needed someone to be there. *(Stands)*

LEADER: " . . . and in prison but you would not take care of me" *(Matt. 25:43c, GNB).*

INTERRUPTER #6: I just wanted a friend to help fill the loneliness. *(Stands)*

LEADER: " 'Then they will answer him,' " "When, Lord, did we ever see you hungry or thirsty or a stranger or naked or sick or in prison, and we would not help you?" ' 'The King will reply,' ' "I tell you, whenever you refused to help one of these least important ones, you refused to help me." ' 'These, then, will be sent off to eternal punishment, but the righteous will go to eternal life' " *(Matt. 25:44-46, GNB). (Pause; realization)* Oh, my goodness, I think I understand now. *(Pause)* Forgive me, Lord. *(Bows head. Freeze.)*

The Road to Bandania
by Matthew Trent Tullos

(Evangelism)

Cast: #1—The Man with Sight, #2—The Girl Who Receives Sight, #3—The Rebel, #4—Rebel's Girlfriend, #5—The Wounded Bandanite, #6—The Cheerleader, #7—The Searcher

In Bandania everyone is blind. They really don't care that they're blind, because they were born with a bandana around their eyes. They don't know anything else. These people are called the Bandanites (Ban-dan-ites).

Some have taken off their bandanas and discovered an incredible light.

The only extra prop needed is a sign saying "Bandania, Land of Pleasure-Straight Ahead." The only extra costume pieces needed are bandanas.

The conclusion of the play makes a smooth transition for an altar call. The greatest challenge on the road to Bandania for the actors is to perform without

sight. This adds to the comedic dimension of the play.

#1: Before I became a Christian, I couldn't understand the idea of Christ dying for what I did wrong. It's as if my eyes were blinded—spiritually blinded. Finally, I was tired of stumbling around in the dark. There are still many people looking for sight. They don't even know it. Sometimes I wish they could see their own blindness. I wonder what would happen if spiritual blindness meant physical blindness. *(Pause)* Hey!! That's the magic of theater. Snap your finger *(He snaps.)* and wishes *can* for a moment become reality!

(#2, The girl who receives sight, walks around alone on stage, stumbling over her own feet. She has a bandana around her eyes. #1 approaches her.)

#1: Can I help you?

#2: Oh, no thanks. I'll make it on my own.

#1: Okay. *(Pause)* But if you need any help, I . . .

#2: Listen, mister, I've already said I'm fine. I don't need you. Okay?

#1: Okay. *(Pause)* But if . . .

#2: Please!

#1 and #2: Okay.

(#2 trips over a sign that says "Bandania, Land of Pleasure Straight Ahead." She falls to the ground, grabs foot, cries in pain.)

#2: A-a-a-h-h-h-!!!

#1: You okay?

#2: Yes, leave me alone.

#1: You're not okay.

#2: I stumbled . . .

#1: Like most Bandanites—

#2: Can you give me a hand?

#1: Sure. *(He helps her up.)*

#2: I'm trying to get to Bandania. Do you know where that is?

#1: Of course. But why do you want to go there?

#2: All my friends are there! It's a land of pleasure! Doesn't everyone want to go?

#1: Not me.

#2: Why not?

#1: It's a lie.

#2: What?

#1: You might have fun for a while, but pretty soon the stumbling and bruises will leave you wounded. *(Pause)* Why are you wearing that bandana?

#2: You say that like you don't have one!

#1: I don't.

#2: You were born with one. Everyone was.

#1: Yep, but I took mine off.

#2: You're kidding?

#1: Nope.

#2: Really?

#1: Yep—If you take off your bandana, you'll have a thing they call . . . SIGHT!!!

#2: You don't really believe in sight, do you?

#1: I not only believe in it, I have it!

#2: Do you still get hurt and stumble?—Run into things?

#1: Sure. But not as often, and I can *see* what I stumbled over and move those things out of the path.

#2: Well, I sure am tired of running into things. And you sound very happy.

#1: I am.

#2: It's a tough decision, but I might as well give it a try.

#1: Great!

#2: Here goes nothing.

#1: No. Here goes everything! *(#2 pulls off the bandana.)*

#2: Wow! It's so bright! *(Squinting her eyes)* I *can* see! I can see *you!* I can see *me!* I can see the path.

#1: Sight is a wonderful gift.

#2: Since sight is true, Bandania must be a lie.

#1: There *is* a place called Bandania, but it's not all it's cracked up to be. It's not a land of pleasure—but rather a land of blindness.

#2: What should I do now?

#1: Come with me. *(He walks in the opposite direction from Bandania.)*

#2: But wait! No one else walks this way.

#1: No Bandanites. But we must.

(#3 enters.)

#2: Look! Someone is walking toward us. He's heading toward Bandania.

(#3, The Rebel, runs into #1.)

#3: Listen, bud. Get out of my way!

#2: Wait a minute! *You* ran into *him!*

#3: Listen, I don't care who ran into whom. I'm late for a party in Bandania. By the way, do you know a short cut?

#1: You'll never make it anywhere.

#3: Oh great. Another smart punk!

#1: You're blind!

#3: You're one of those . . . *(Sarcastically)* fanatics—A believer in sight. I just can't seem to get away from you guys!

#1: You're not content!

#3: I'm having a blast.

#1: But you're not happy.

#3: Who is?

#2: We are.

#3: You're not happy. You're brainwashed. You just *think* you have sight.

#2: No, we really *do!* It's real.

#1: It's everlasting!

(#4, Rebel's Girlfriend enters trying to catch up with #3.)

#4: Hey! I said wait for me!

#3: Sorry, babe. I just didn't want to be late.

#4: Who were you talking to? Are they going to Bandania?

#1: No—

#2: Not anymore.

#4: Come on! Join the party!!

#3: It's no use. They believe in a thing *they* call sight.

#4: Lies! Fairy tales! Myths! Don't believe them. They're just silly dreamers.

#3: They seem to have something that we don't have. I might just take their challenge.

#2: Great!

#4: All they have is a good imagination. They probably threw away their bandanas because they weren't as . . . attractive as some of the new bandanas on the market these days.

#1: Everyone was born with a bandana. The secret is taking them off your . . .

#4: Taking them off your *face.* What a joke! *(To #3)* They believe that under the bandana are things called eyes! *(Laughs)*

#2: All I know is that I once was blind, but now I . . .

#4: See. Sure, honey. Everybody was born with a bandana. It's just that some are . . . well, you know . . . better than others. For example, I would never be caught dead with a polyester bandana. Mine is 100 percent cotton, monogrammed, and heavily starched. Brand names only, please. I'm worth it. Come on, sweetheart!

#3: Go ahead, babe. I want to talk to them about this sight.

#4: It's now or never!

#3: But I . . .

#4: Now!

(#3 walks toward #1 and #2, then reluctantly turns back to #4. They exit quickly.)

#1: Many want sight, but few ever dare to receive it!

#2: What do you think will happen to him?

#1: It's hard to say. Hopefully there'll be more encounters with people like us along his journey.

#2: I hope that those with sight will have courage to speak to him.

#1: Look!

(Enter #5, The Wounded Bandanite. She is groping, stumbling.)

#2: She looks like she needs sight.

#1: Everybody *needs* sight. Some are just more used to blindness than others.

#2: Hey, do you need help?

#5: *(Crying)* Does it look like it? *(#2 is speechless.)* Look, just leave me alone. You don't know who you're dealing with. Do you have sight?

#2: Yes.

#5: That's an even better reason to leave me alone.

#2: Don't you want sight?

#5: Of course I do—but people with sight are always condemning me.

#2: I won't condemn you.

#5: That's what they all say until they find out about my scars and bruises I have from being blind. They laugh or condemn.

#2: Look, I don't know who these peo-ple are, but we're not . . .

#5: Just leave me alone. Okay? *(#5 rushes off stage.)*

#2: Wait! I'm not like them! *(To #1)* Why didn't she trust me?

#1: There are many people who have sight, but they develop pride. They become nearsighted. They use their sight to condemn the blind and laugh at the scars and bruises of the Bandanites.

(#6, The Cheerleader runs across the stage)

#1: Wait!

#2: Hey, where are you going?

#6: I don't have time to talk. Cheerleading practice is in five minutes.

#2: What about after?

#6: The honor society is having a banquet at seven, and then the football team is . . .

#1: Don't you have time?

#6: For what?

#2: Sight!

#6: To be honest, no. Plus, my boyfriend loves my bandana. I don't know how he'd like me if I took it off. Besides, I'm having so much fun!

#2: The way you're running around, without sight, you're bound to run off a cliff or into a wall.

#6: I guess that's the chance I'll take. Thanks for being so concerned, but really—I'm doing great. *(#6 exits.)*

#1: I have a feeling she's more doomed than anyone we've met today.

#2: Why's that? She seemed confident and well-adjusted.

#1: The confident ones always seem to fall harder.

#2: Those kind of Bandanites just make me want to throw up my hands and quit talking about sight.

#1: Yeah, sometimes they make you feel like sight is not worth it . . . but there are always a few waiting, hoping to find out. So we've got to keep on. If we don't who will?

(#1 and #2 exit in the opposite direction from the Bandanites.)

(#7, The Searcher, enters from the direction that the Bandanites exited.)

#7: Hey, is there anyone here? *(Yelling)* They told me you would be here. The Bandanites said that you believe in sight. Are you still here? I'm blind. What is sight? Where are you? *(Pause)* I suppose the Bandanites were right. There is no sight . . . only the darkness of our minds.

(Actors return to the stage, frozen in active positions illustrating their life and blindness. #1 enters and speaks as he moves around the frozen actors.)

#1: How will they know if we don't tell them? They will continue to stumble in darkness. Maybe you are spiritually blind. If you are, the message is that Jesus Christ can open your eyes. He came not to make bad people good, but to make the dead live and the blind to see.

Wait on the Lord
by Gail Blanton

(Discussion, Bible Study)
Characters: 1 male, 1 female
(Grandfatherly type seated in a chair. Linda enters left, crosses to Man)

LINDA: Hello there. Uh . . . can we talk?

MAN: Sure, Linda.

LINDA: *(Sits on floor by Man and rests her arms on His knees, using some variation of this pose throughout. Sometimes she looks at audience, her head resting on her arms. Sometimes her head is up, but she seems to be looking into space. Sometimes she looks at the Man, symbolic of prayer, but not a formal prayer posture.)* Oh, thanks. You know, You're the only one I can have any kind of meaningful conversation with anymore.

MAN: Is that right?

LINDA: I mean, nobody will *talk* to me. All I get are these enlightening little comments like "hmmmm" and "really" and "well"! Good grief, that's not conversation. I need some feedback.

MAN: I'm sorry, honey.

LINDA: I mean, are people too busy or just not interested, or scared of sharing their feelings, of involvement?

MAN: Probably.

LINDA: Even Mom and Dad, for goodness' sake. I mean, they're already pretty involved with me. Anyway, I'm glad You're here because I need to know how You feel about things and what You think I should do.

MAN: I'm listening.

LINDA: Well, first there's Kevin. He asks my opinion about something and I tell him. But if it's not the same as his opinion he says I'm arguing. If we're going somewhere and I give him directions he says he doesn't need my help. But if he misses a turn, he says, "Well why didn't you tell me?" You understand the mind of man, right? How can I please him?

Then there's Carla. I don't know if she would make a good roommate. There's something about her that I can't quite

49

put my finger on, but then I'm always too critical of people and no one is perfect and I like her a lot. So, should I forget it or give it a chance?

And what about that part-time job? Offered to me right out of the blue like that, it's bound to be right, isn't it? Well, I mean, not necessarily, but You know I need the money. But I'd probably have to drop one of my classes and then I'd graduate late, and timing can mean everything. Oh, I don't know. What should I do?

And I sure do wish You'd tell me how to show my Christian witness without turning people off. I mean, if I offend them it would be better not to say anything in the first place, right? So how can I make my way of life seem attractive rather than high-us pious?

Oh, and that problem at the church. You know the one I mean. Whose side should I take, or should I keep quiet? Whose side are You on?

And then there's Nanny Taylor. Should I ask for her healing or has her time come to go on home? I really don't know what to say. What do *You* say at a time like that? Well, that's about it for today, I guess. I sure do hope You have some answers for me. *(Pauses momentarily, long enough for Man to smile and open His mouth to speak; then quickly jumps up)* Well, it's been great talking with You. I gotta run. Bye.

MAN: *(Sits with his mouth still open and a gesture of reaching out as Linda exists; then shakes His head sadly.)*

READER: "Wait on the Lord" *(Ps. 27:14).*

" 'Incline your ear and come to Me. Lis-

ten, that you may live' " *(Isa. 55:3, NASB).*

" 'He who has ears to hear, let him hear' " *(Matt. 11:15, NASB).*

Trackers
by Rod Payne

(Missions)

Characters: 2

(As the lights come up one character is looking at something on the ground. Another character approaches.)

PERSON #1: Let's see . . . it looks like they start here out of nowhere and just keep going. Man, I wonder if they really could be.

PERSON #2: Could be what?

PERSON #1: Oh, hi. I didn't see you come up.

PERSON #2: Yeah, I could tell. What're you looking at?

PERSON #1: These footprints on the ground here. I was just walking around when I saw these footprints and a little note scratched out here in the dirt.

PERSON #2: What did the note say?

PERSON #1: It was just words really; they said "Footsteps of Jesus."

PERSON #2: What?!

PERSON #1: I didn't think you'd believe me. Look for yourself. I'm gonna follow these footprints.

PERSON #2: Sure, these are footprints of Jesus. Next thing you're gonna tell me is the Last Supper was held over there at McDonald's.

PERSON #1: They seem to be moving in this direction.

PERSON #2: Wait a minute. This is probably a prank. You're not really gonna fall for this bit, are you?

PERSON #1: They're going over here near this old house.

PERSON #2: Wait, I'm coming with you. I want to see how this gag turns out.

PERSON #1: Man, look at this family. There's got to be six kids and it looks like they all share this one room. They don't even have enough beds for everybody.

PERSON #2: Probably their own fault. You know a lot of these people don't like to work. Anyway what would Jesus be doing here?

PERSON #1: I don't know. The footprints lead on this way. They're going . . . they're going over to Kelly's Bar.

PERSON #2: See, I told you this was some kind of practical joke. What would Jesus be doing in a bar?

PERSON #1: I don't know. Hey, the footprints leave the bar and head over to that house.

PERSON #2: That's probably where the kid lives who pulled this prank.

PERSON #1: There's a kid inside all right, but he doesn't look like he's enjoying any joke.

PERSON #2: Maybe he's crying because his folks caught him making those footprints all over the place.

PERSON #1: No, look in this other window.

PERSON #2: What are you; some kind of peeping Tom?

PERSON #1: Shh, listen . . . they're talking about who's going to get what in their divorce. It looks like the husband is packing some kind of bag.

PERSON #2: Man, let's get out of here before some cop drives by and sees us looking in somebody's window. Even if there was something to these footprints, what would Jesus be doing here? I know He didn't go in for divorce and that stuff.

PERSON #1: I don't know, but it looks like the prints keep going over to the . . . hey, it looks like the footprints are headed for that church.

PERSON #2: Man, what an elaborate hoax to try and get people to come to church.

PERSON #1: They're not going to the front door, though, they're headed for the side.

PERSON #2: What do you suppose the guy was looking at here? There's nothing but a stained glass window and some seats with padding on 'em.

PERSON #1: I don't know. Let's see, it looks like they keep going around to the back of the church building.

PERSON #2: Maybe the guy who made the prints wanted to sneak in the back way.

PERSON #1: But the prints don't stop at the back door. Wait, what are these other marks in the dirt. The footprints don't look the same either.

PERSON #2: This is weird, man, it looks like those could be impressions made by . . . by knees. It looks like the guy was kneeling here or something.

PERSON #1: Yeah, but the footprints don't end here, they're taking off again.

PERSON #2: I don't get it. If this were some kind of practical joke why wouldn't the steps of "Jesus" end up at the church? That's where they're supposed to keep Him 'n' all.

PERSON #1: I don't know. It looks like they keep going so I'm gonna follow 'em for awhile. Wanna come?

PERSON #2: Nah, you go on. Whoever is making these footprints is going to a lot of places respectable people would never go.

(Blackout)

The Two Trees of Christmas
by Dan Kirkland

(Christmas or Easter)

Characters: 2 males

(Man stands at one side of the stage beside a Christmas tree. God stands beneath a large wooden cross.)

GOD: You are in pain my child?

MAN: Yes, God. I hurt so much.

GOD: Is it because of that tree? *(God points toward the Christmas tree.)*

MAN: Yes, God. The memories are too painful to bear. It was one week ago when my son and I cut down that tree.

GOD: Do you see that tree? *(Pointing toward the cross)*

MAN: Yes, Lord.

GOD: One of My children cut it down too.

MAN: But God my boy died yesterday. I hurt so much. I ache. When I see that tree I cry. I remember my son.

GOD: I know. You loved your son. He died. The tree is a symbol of his death for you.

MAN: Yes, God.

GOD: That tree over there *(Pointing toward cross)* they hung My Son upon it. It makes Me grieve when I think of His pain *(God bends over and pretends to pull a spike out of the lower section of the cross.)*, His sorrows *(God pretends to pull a spike out of the left cross bar.)*, His trag-edy *(Pulling the final spike out)*. *(God now reaches down at the front of the cross and pretends to pick up and hold the body of Christ.)* But, His body is now the church. *(Pretending to hand over the body to the congregation.)*

MAN: *(A bit angry)* Yes, God. And I have peeked behind the veil of His church and seen His body. And it is mangled and torn, and cold, and . . . dead. Resurrect it Lord.

GOD: You resurrect it. You are My hands.

MAN: I cannot resurrect Your church. It needs reformation and cleansing.

GOD: It is you who needs resurrection and cleansing. I have peeked within your heart and it is mangled and torn, and cold and . . . dead.

MAN: *(Less angry, but emotional)* But God You took my boy.

GOD: *(Very patient and kind)* And you took Mine. You looked at that tree. *(Pointing toward the cross)* You accepted My Son. But, now you say He is dead.

MAN: But my tree God, *(Pointing toward the tree)* reminds me of my son's death.

GOD: May it remind you of My Son's birth.

MAN: But Your tree God, reminds me of Your Son's death. *(Pointing toward the cross)*

GOD: Let it remind you of His life, His glory, His wonder . . . Your salvation.

MAN: But God, I look into my heart and I see that You are right. It is mangled and torn and cold, and . . . dead. How do I breathe life back into it?

GOD: I can do it. Be still and know that I am God. Trust Me. Trust your son to

Me. He is safe. He is with Me. He has life. But, I have left My Son with you. Inside your soul. And you say you have peeked behind the veil and He is dead. Did you kill Him?

MAN: No, Lord. It was me that I saw, not Him. He is alive. He is inside me and inside all of these people *(Pointing toward congregation)*. If He dies it is because we all die. If He lives it is because we live.

GOD: Put your eyes on the right tree this season. It is the tree of the cross where Jesus died for you. It is a glorious tree where you get new life. Celebrate His life as you look at your tree. *(Raising right arm so that hand is where spike would be)* Celebrate your new life in Him when you look at my tree. *(Raising left arm so that hand is where spike would be)*

MAN: Thank You, Father. I love You.

GOD: And I have always loved you. This much. *(With arms still stretched across crossbars of the cross God allows His head to drop as if He has died.)*

(Congregation is then led in "Silent Night, Holy Night" a capella.)

What Kind of Christian Are You?
by Sharla Hester Condren

(Youth, VBS, worship, discussion)
Cast: Reporter, Loving Christian, Happy Christian, Religious Christian, Worried Christian, Uncaring Christian, New Christian
Props: Hand-held, cordless microphone
Setting: Church. The characters, except the reporter, are seated in various places in the congregation.

REPORTER: *(Standing at front of church)* Good evening/morning. We are here at *(name of church)* to ask the question . . . What kind of Christian are you? *(The Loving Christian starts to sing, "Jesus Loves Me." Reporter walks over to Loving Christian.)*

REPORTER: Excuse me, but can I ask you a question?

LOVING CHRISTIAN: *(Standing)* Sure, I would love for you to ask me a question!

REPORTER: What kind of Christian are you?

LOVING CHRISTIAN: I am a loving Christian. I love Jesus and Jesus loves me. I love my church, I love my Bible, I love the pews, I love all the people. Smile, God loves you. I even love you! *(Loving Christian sits down. Happy Christian begins to sing, "If you're happy and you know it, clap your hands." Reporter walks over to Happy Christian.)*

REPORTER: Would you answer a question?

HAPPY CHRISTIAN: *(Standing)* I'd be happy to!

REPORTER: What kind of Christian are you?

HAPPY CHRISTIAN: I'm happy to say, I'm a happy Christian! Church makes me happy. I'm always happy. Put on a happy face. A happy Christian is a happy person.

(Happy Christian sits down. Religious Christian shouts "Praise the Lord!" Reporter walks over to Religious Christian.)

REPORTER: Excuse me, but could you answer a question?

RELIGIOUS CHRISTIAN: *(Standing)* Hallelujah! What's the question?

REPORTER: What kind of Christian are you?

RELIGIOUS CHRISTIAN: Praise the Lord, I'm a religious Christian! Bless you my brother/sister for asking! God is my co-pilot. Amen, Hallelujah! I'll be praying for you friend. Praise the Lord! *(Religious Christian sits down. Worried Christian starts saying, "Oh my goodness, oh my goodness." Reporter walks over to Worried Christian.)*

REPORTER: Could I ask you a question?

WORRIED CHRISTIAN: *(Standing)* I'm a worried Christian. I'm worried about the preacher. I'm worried about the ceiling falling in. If I don't worry about the church, I'm worried no one will. Worry is my life. I'm even worried about God!

(Worried Christian sits down. Uncaring Christian starts talking out loud to someone on her/his pew. Reporter walks to Uncaring Christian.)

REPORTER: Excuse me, but could I ask you a question?

UNCARING CHRISTIAN: *(Standing)* I don't care.

REPORTER: What kind of Christian are you?

UNCARING CHRISTIAN: I am an uncaring Christian. I don't care about anyone here. I don't care about the music or the preaching. I use to care, but I don't anymore. Hey, I don't care to talk to you anymore, either.

(Uncaring Christian sits down. New Christian gets up and starts to leave. Reporter stops him/her.)

REPORTER: Excuse me, but could you answer a question?

NEW CHRISTIAN: *(Stops)* I guess so.

REPORTER: What kind of Christian are you?

NEW CHRISTIAN: I don't think I am a Christian.

REPORTER: Why not?

NEW CHRISTIAN: Well, I just got saved last month, or at least I thought I was saved, but after listening to all those other people who are Christians, I'm not sure. I'm just not sure.

(New Christian continues to leave. Reporter returns to front.)

REPORTER: Our time is up for tonight/today, but we may be back next week to again ask someone, maybe even you, the question . . . What kind of Christian are you?

Impress Who?
by Gail Blanton

(Discussion Bible Study)

Characters: 1 male, 1 female

(Man and woman enter talking, as if in the middle of a conversation begun off-stage. Could enter from sides or back of sanctuary. Others "planted" on ends of pews could try to hush them by saying "shhh," "we're trying to worship here," etc.)

SHE: I'm really going to try to impress him, you know? I thought I'd buy a new outfit to wear—a really classy one.

HE: He won't pay any attention.

SHE: Well I think he'll notice that I've taken good care of my—uh—body.

HE: Oh, sure, but someone like him expects that, really.

SHE: Some people say my hair's my best point, though. I was going to fix it in a style that shows off how long and full it is.

HE: I think he's already noticed how much hair you have.

SHE: Oh really? Well I hope he appreciates a good mind as well.

HE: Of course he does. But you couldn't come close to his knowledge, you know.

SHE: Boy, are you negative or what?

HE: No, just let me tell you how to approach him.

SHE: I heard he was big on social work. I'm going to make sure he knows I work one night a week at the crisis intervention center. Of course I give to charity, and I spend my Thanksgiving holiday working on the serving line at the soup kitchen. Do you think that would impress him? That's pretty good, don't you think?

HE: Sure it is, but . . .

SHE: But don't get me wrong. I don't let that take away from my job performance. Last year I was chosen employee of the year.

HE: No doubt hard work is commendable, but . . .

SHE: Oh, I get it. He's the creative type, right?

HE: Definitely.

SHE: Artistic perhaps? Well what a coincidence. I've been painting for years. Landscapes mostly.

HE: He paints the most beautiful sunsets you can imagine. Sunrises too, for that matter. Storms, mountains, oceans.

SHE: I see. Well perhaps he wouldn't think mine were all that good then. There must be something about me that would impress him. Probably if you just told him what a nice girl I am. Every-body says so. There should be a premium on them—not that many left in the world.

HE: I guess not. But a lot of nice girls are interested in him.

SHE: Oh, I get it now. I might have known—money. That's the price of everything. He's looking for someone with lots of resources. Is that it?

HE: No, he's independently wealthy.

SHE: Boy, this guy has everything, doesn't he?

HE: So they say.

SHE: Then how in the world can I ever impress him?

HE: You can't.

SHE: (*Hurrying down steps, sits in front pew.*) Oh, forget it.

HE: Right.

SHE: I give up.

HE: Good. (*Beginning to move toward her*) Now you can really get to know each other.

SHE: I said I give up.

HE: That's all he ever wanted from you. (*Takes Bible from altar and turns its pages as he goes to stand in front of her. He turns the Bible toward her, points to a verse and smiles; then sits beside her as if explaining the Scripture. Fade lights or fade in appropriate music.*)

The Potter and the Clay
by Don Blackley

(Bible study, youth, discussion)
Cast: Potter, Voice of the Clay, Narrator

A potter stands at a work table with a large lump of clay in front of him. He begins to busily work the lump of clay, molding, shaping, pounding. As he works his pounding becomes more firm. The clay begins to groan and grumble (offstage voice). Have fun with the action as the potter threatens to hit the lump and then waits—Each time he pounds the lump, the clay will react. Finally the clay takes all it can and . . .

CLAY: (*Offstage actor needs to be able to see Potter.*) Quit poking me!

POTTER: (*Dropping clay*) Who said that? (*Looking around*)

CLAY: I did!

POTTER: (*Looking at lump*) Who did?

CLAY: I did. And I've got some more to say too!

POTTER: Well, of all the crazy things...

CLAY: Not so crazy. I'm just tired of you pounding around on me.

POTTER: Yeah, but clay can't talk!

CLAY: I just never wanted to talk before. Up until now everything was fine. I just used to lay around the swamp and have a good time making little gurgly sounds.

POTTER: Well, things are tough all over. (*Starts kneading clay.*) But, I've promised Rebecca I would make her a grease jar.

CLAY: A grease jar!

POTTER: That's what she needs, and that's what you're going to be.

CLAY: But I wanted to be a beautiful VASE (*pronounced vahse*)!

POTTER: A VASE (*pronounced vahse*) already—not even content to just be a flower pot.

CLAY: Well, isn't that my right as an individual to determine my own destiny?

POTTER: Now listen clay, who do you think is in charge here?

CLAY: Well, I was just . . .

POTTER: Get this one thing straight . . . I is the potter. You is the pottee! And if I need for you to be a grease jar that's what you'll be.

CLAY: Final?

POTTER: Final!

CLAY: Oh well, I guess I wouldn't have liked being a vase anyway. I hear that those rose thorns can drive you crazy in a flower arrangement.

POTTER: That's the spirit, Greasy! (*He freezes in position.*)

NARRATOR: "Here is another message to Jeremiah from the Lord: Go down to the shop where clay pots and jars are made and I will talk to you there. I did as he told me, and found the potter working at his wheel. But the jar that he was forming didn't turn out as he wished, so he kneaded it into a lump and started again. Then the Lord said: O Israel, can't I do to you as this potter has done to his clay? As the clay is in the potter's hand, so are you in my hand" (*Jer. 18:1-6, TLB*).

(*Exit*)

Hypocrite!
by Sharla Hester Condren

(Youth, VBS, Bible study)

Cast: Visitor, Hypocrite #1, Hypocrite #2, Person #3, Person #4, Person #5, Sunday School Teacher

Props: Chairs lined in three rows of three chairs each, Bible for Visitor

Setting: A Sunday School classroom

(*Visitor enters and sits down on second row of chairs. Hypocrite #1 and Hypocrite #2 enter and approach the Visitor.*)

HYPOCRITE #1: Excuse me, but you

are sitting in my seat.

(*Visitor looks at Hypocrite #1 in a confused state.*)

HYPOCRITE #2: We sit here all the time. Everybody knows that, but you are a visitor, so I guess you wouldn't know that.

HYPOCRITE #1: (*Leans over and points to the back of the chair in front of Visitor.*) Look, you can see where I carved my initials next to the little heart and the little cross.

(*Visitor moves to the row in front of them, where she can hear everything that is said. She reacts with appropriate facial expressions.*)

(*Hypocrite #1 and Hypocrite #2 sit down, Person #3 enters the front of the room.*)

HYPOCRITE #2: Look at her. (*Points to Person #3.*) Have you ever seen such an awful mess of hair in your life?

HYPOCRITE #1: It looks worse than my dog's!

(*Person #3 nears them.*)

PERSON #3: Hello, how are you today?

HYPOCRITE #2: Well, I am just fine and you look terrific. I just love your hair fixed like that!

HYPOCRITE #1: Every time I see you, your hair looks great.

PERSON #3: That's what I like about you. You are always so nice.

(*Person #3 sits down in row behind them. Person #4 enters the front of the room.*)

HYPOCRITE #1: Well, would you look at what she is wearing! That outfit makes her look like she weighs 200 pounds!

HYPOCRITE #2: Yes, and that color makes her look sick!

(*Person #4 nears them.*)

PERSON #4: Good morning.

HYPOCRITE #1: Well, how in the world did you lose so much weight? You look great!

HYPOCRITE #2: Yes you do and that is definitely your color. You should wear it all the time!

PERSON #4: You are always so nice to me.

(*Person #4 sits down on back row. Person #5 enters front of room.*)

HYPOCRITE #1: Look there she is—Miss Homecoming USA. She thinks she won because everyone likes her and because of some great personality.

HYPOCRITE #2: The only reason she won is because she flirts with all the guys in school.

(*Person #5 nears them.*)

PERSON #5: Hi! How are things going?

HYPOCRITE #1: Congratulations on winning Homecoming Queen. I thought you were the best choice. I voted for you.

HYPOCRITE #2: You have such a great personality. The other girls thought if they flirted with the guys they would win, but not you.

PERSON #5: That's what I like about you. You are always so nice.

(*Person #5 sits down on back row. Sunday School Teacher enters.*)

SUNDAY SCHOOL TEACHER: Good morning girls. Our lesson today has to do with passing judgment on others. Do any of you know a passage of Scripture that applies?

(*Hypocrite #1 raises hand.*)

HYPOCRITE #1: In Matthew 7:1-2 it says, "Do not judge lest you be judged. For in the way you judge, you will be judged; and by your standard of measure, it will be measured to you" *(NASB)*.

(Hypocrite #2 raises hand.)

HYPOCRITE #2: In Romans 14:13 it says, "Therefore let us not judge one another any more, but rather determine this—not to put an obstacle or a stumbling block in a brother's way" *(NASB)*.

(The Visitor, who has been looking through the Bible, gets up, walks toward the door, and then turns around. She opens the Bible and begins to read.)

VISITOR: "How can you say to your brother, 'Let me take the speck out of your eye,' and behold, the log is in your own eye? You hypocrite, first take the log out of your own eye, and then you will see clearly to take the speck out of your brother's eye" *(Matt. 7:4-5, NASB).*

(Visitor closes Bible and leaves.)

(Hypocrite #1 and Hypocrite #2 exchange confused looks.)

HYPOCRITE #1: The devil always sends someone to cause trouble.

HYPOCRITE #2: Amen.

A Strong-Armed Lady Named Annie
by Tom and Delores Eggleston

(Home Missions)

Characters: 1 male, 1 female

FLOYD: Good morning, Miss Delores, how you doin'?

DELORES: Oh, I'm find Floyd. Thanks for cleaning up my office.

FLOYD: Well, I'm just doin' my job, ya know. That's what custodial engineers get paid for. Hey, what are you so busy doin', anyway?

DELORES: I'm gettin' ready to do a monologue in church about Annie Armstrong.

FLOYD: It sounds like a disease—mono-logue, mono, mono . . .

DELORES: No, Floyd, it's just a little talk about home missions.

FLOYD: Hey, I know a lot about home missions. That's when missionaries goes into people's homes, right?

DELORES: Well, that's close. See Annie Armstrong was this lady who . . .

FLOYD: I know her. Ain't she a member of your church? You know, that tall lady who teaches third grade Sunday School, right?

DELORES: No, Floyd, she's dead.

FLOYD: You don't mean it. When's the funeral?

DELORES: You don't understand, Annie Armstrong died in the early 1900's. She's really known as the mother of home missions. She helped start Woman's Missionary Union and much of the work of the Home Mission Board.

FLOYD: Oh, I must of had the wrong Annie! You mean she started a mercenary union for women? She wasn't one of those woman's libbers, was she?

DELORES: No, Floyd, it was a missionary union and she wasn't a women's libber. In fact, she had some pretty strong feelings about women's roles in church. For example, she wouldn't even speak before a group of men because she thought it was improper.

FLOYD: My kind of lady! What else did she do?

DELORES: Well, she became concerned about all the internationals she saw coming into the ports of her hometown of Baltimore, Maryland. She encouraged the Home Mission Board to provide a ministry for internationals.

FLOYD: Yeah, those Yankees need all the help they can get.

DELORES: Floyd, you don't understand. I'm not talking about Northerners, I'm talking about immigrants—people from Germany, England, and all parts of the world.

FLOYD: Wow, you mean to tell me she loved ALL those foreigners.

DELORES: Yes, she had a great love and concern for all people regardless of race. She lived in Baltimore all of her life, but she did travel to other places trying to get mission work started. She even went out to Oklahoma to visit an Indian school that her uncle helped start.

FLOYD: They didn't scalp her, did they?!

DELORES: No, Floyd, they were very nice to her. In fact it was her love and concern for Indians that started Miss Annie thinking that women in the churches should begin organizing to pray for Home Missions and give money to support missions.

FLOYD: Ain't that something?! How'd they do?

DELORES: Pretty good. As a result of Miss Annie's efforts we now have WMU in our Southern Baptist churches. We have special home and foreign mission offerings at Easter time and Christmas to raise money for missions. Our home missions goal this year is _____ million dollars and our church's goal is _____ dollars.

FLOYD: You got to be kiddin'?! Boy, that's a lot of money. Reckon, I could get a loan from that Miss Annie offerin'? I got a pickup truck that needs lots of work!

DELORES: No, I'm afraid not, Floyd. All the money goes to home missions and missionaries. They really need our help. Miss Annie found that missionaries were living in poverty and were lonely. She started writing to tell them she was praying for them and trying to get more support for better salaries. Why, in one year she wrote more than 17,000 letters.

FLOYD: Talk about writer's cramp . . . know what I mean? Well, I sure did learn a lot about that strong-armed lady, Miss Annie. It makes me wanna go sign up.

DELORES: Sign up for what?!

FLOYD: Sign up to be a missionary. Hey, maybe they're some other folks that'd like to be missionaries, too. (Goes into audience.) Hey, you look like you'd make a good missionary. You do too. Listen, ya'll meet me in the church parking lot at 12:30 sharp and we'll go sign up! Be there or be square!

DELORES: Floyd, you're too much!

Dramables
by Matthew Trent Tullos

The following interpretations are modern dramatic parables, or, "dramables." These can be performed together as a dramatic sermon or they can be performed separately as illustrations leading into a teaching time. Most of them are also en-

Prologue

#1: Many, many years ago
The prophets and preachers cried:
#2: Oh God, where are You?
When are You coming?
#1: Others thought God had died.
#2: Where is a miracle? Where is a sign?
You know we asked for a king.
#1: He doesn't have to be all that rich,
Just some jewels
and a nice diamond ring!
#2: If we had a king,
we'd conquer the earth.
#1: Show us a star:
He'll be king at His birth.
#2: We'll spread the good news.
#1: He'll be king of the Jews.
#2: We'll give Him a home,
#1: And He'll conquer Rome.
#2: We'll love Him,
#1: We'll serve Him,
#1, #2: You know we deserve Him.
#2: With a purple robe,
and a crown on His head,
We'll worship Him even after He's dead.
#1: But we won't need to die.
He'll be part of your spirit.
When death knocks at His door,
He won't even hear it.
#2: With hearts open wide,
this is our plea.
It's what we need most, don't you agree?
#1: The world looked on.
A pauper appeared—Jesus Christ.
Some thought Him just a wee bit weird.
#2: He didn't have a wife or trade,

Not a hammer, nail, or even a spade.
#1: Yet He would build a house so wide
That all who entered found room inside.
With a foundation of faith
And walls made of love,
A roof made of hope
Sheltered Him from above.
#2: Now this home was not built
in one single place.
It was found in the hearts
that saw God in His face.
#1: He wasn't the most attractive
of men.
#2: His hair was too long,
#1: His body too thin.
#2: But people traveled mile upon mile
To hear Him speak
and to see Him smile.
#1: He wasn't a man
of difficult words.
His language was simple
as lilies and birds.
#2: The children were first
to call Him king.
For He loved to tell stories,
smile, and sing.
#1: So now we present
these tales of today,
#2: For if Christ were here,
He might speak this way.

Parable of Prayer

#1: Our Lord was praying
in a certain place
and when He stopped,
one of His disciples said to Him—
#2: Jesus teach us to pray.
#1: And He said to them:
#2: Men shouldn't be actors
when talking to God.
When people do this,

He thinks it's quite odd.
And when you pray find a private place.
Then you will feel
God's warm, holy face.
God knows everything you need,
So why should your prayers
be full of greed?
Make your prayers honest and true,
And when you pray, pray as I do.
Our Father in heaven,
I want to praise Your name.
#1: May Your wishes be done on earth
and heaven the same.
#2: We ask You to give us
the things we need,
When we till the earth
and plant the seed.
#1: Forgive us
when we don't do what You ask,
#2: While we forgive those
who might fail *us* in a task.
#1: Keep us clear of the evil one.
He tries to tell us what should be done.
Help us, Dear Father,
to tell him to leave.
It's so easy to do
when it's You we believe.
#2: And it is to You
#1, #2: Our praises we bring.
#2: For we know, Dear Father,
You own everything.
#1: Dear God, it is You
that we want to see.
#1, #2: We love You,
#1: Our Father, so let it be.
#2: And He said to them,
"Is God like this?"
#1: Knock, knock.
#2: Who's there?
#1: Darlene.
#2: Darlene who?

#1: Darlene Tu——.
Hey, this isn't a joke!
#2: I hope not—it's after midnight.
This better be a good one.
#1: Please, open the door.
It's cold out here.
#2: What do you want?
#1: My grandmother from Toledo
just dropped in,
and I'm fresh out of bread.
Can I borrow a loaf?
#2: Does this look like a *7-11*?
#1: Please? (*Freeze*)
#2: (*To audience*) Now really . . . do you
think I'm going to leave her out in the
cold without giving her a loaf of bread?
What a sad sight—Darlene and her
grandmother from Toledo going to
bed—supperless!
#1: Matt! Open up!
#2: So because of her boldness,
persistence, and longsuffering—
#1: You betcha—
#2: I will grant her request.
#1: Now, if Matt in all his sinful,
fleshly, uncleanliness . . .
#2: Now wait, that's pouring it on
a little thick, don't you think?
#1: In comparison to Christ—
#1, #2: (*Together*)
#2: Yep, I am.
#1: Yep, you are.
#1: As I was saying, if Matt can understand how to give good things to me,
how much more will your heavenly Father give good things to *you*?
#2: Therefore, ask, ask,
#1: And keep on asking,
#1, #2: And it will be given unto you.
#2: Seek, seek,
#1: And keep on seeking,

#1, #2: And you will find.
#1: Knock, knock.
#2: Who's there?
#1: Cut it out! Knock,
#2: And keep on knocking.
#1, #2: And it will be opened unto you.
#1: Do not ask,
#2: "What are we to eat?"
#1: Or
#2: "What are we to drink?"
#1: Isn't life more important than food or clothes? Look at the birds of the air. (*#2 pantomimes a bird.*) They don't sow or reap, or store away earthly treasures in barns, and yet your heavenly Father feeds them.
#2: *(As bird)* Caw! Caw!
#1: How much more will your heavenly Father feed you?
#2: And look at the lilies of the field. (*#1 pantomimes flower.*) They do not labor or spin. (*#1 begins to spin.*) They *don't* spin . . .
#1: Oops . . . sorry!
#2: Yet Solomon in all his glory was not dressed as one of these. So whom should we seek?
#1: What should we ask?
#2: Where should we knock?
#1: Here is the key—
#2: Seek first the kingdom of God,
#1: And His righteousness,
#1, #2: And all these things will be added unto you!

The Lost Dime

#1: Jesus loved all types of sinners.
He would heal broken bones
and make kingly beginners.
The preachers scorned,
#2: To be righteous and fit

You'll have to be careful
where you eat and sit.
#1: But Jesus replied—
#2: With your fancy clothes
and your self-righteous frown,
Your nose cuts the air
as you walk through the town.
I eat and drink with sinners, that's true.
Because God did not come for the clean, holy few.
You just need religious respect.
But in the end, it's you God will correct.
God seeks the sinner like I'm doing now.
He doesn't even ask who, why, or how.
#1: *(Mimes part of old woman.)*
Like a poor old woman
who has lost her dime,
She searched and searched
with no notice of time.
Next to her couch, under the bed,
She looked through her house
'til her eyes turned red.
She cried many tears
for the money she lost.
She wanted to find it no matter the cost.
Into her dresser she started to look.
Behind all the chairs, inside an old book.
She even searched
through her pots and pans.
Through all the trash
in her garbage cans.
She fell to her bed in bitter dismay
and cried—
#1: Where's the dime I lost today?
#2: But she got up and searched
for the money again.
She felt sure she could find it.
She wouldn't give in.
Then from under the carpet,
guess what she found?
#1: The coin!

#2: She proclaimed
with a loud, joyful sound.
She then ran to her friends,
who rejoiced in her find.
Leaving all her worries
and sorrows behind.
#1: God is that old woman
who has lost His dear treasure.
To find a lost soul
gives Him much pleasure.
#2: Like a father who patiently waits
for his runaway son.
#1: Like a shepherd who leaves
his entire flock to find one.
#2: God's heart is searching
both night and day
To find lonely people
who have lost their way.
He reaches into souls of despair,
And carries them home
with arms of care.

The Preacher and the Farmer

#1: There once was a church
so clean and cute.
The preacher walked in
in a beautiful suit.
He walked through the door
and down the aisle.
He greeted all the people
with a big phony smile.
He spoke to others
who wore fancy clothes.
He didn't care for the poor, I suppose.
Off in the corner was a smelly old man.
The people in town
called him Poor Farmer Dan.
They wanted to throw
that man out in the street.
"His hair was not combed.
No shoes on his feet."

But it was late. Soon church would start.
And to cause a big ruckus
would not be too smart.
They sang a song and then stood to pray.
So with eyes to the heavens,
the preacher spoke this way.
#2: Oh, God in heaven,
Thou dost know
The pain and conflict down below.
Thou who makest all,
winter, spring, summer, fall,
Bless Thou thee, and bless Thou he
(Looking toward Dan)
Who sinneth before Thy very sight,
An causeth me with all my might
To pray that Thou wilt spare his soul
And make him someday surely whole.
For Thou knowest where he goest,
And Thou must weep to see the heap
Of sins, transgressions, lies, and hate
Upon whose judgment he'll await.
So in short this is my plea,
In damnation, better him than me!
#1: God was sad. He loved ol' Dan.
Dan worked hard. He was quite a man.
Now Farmer Dan never
prayed out loud.
He was a little shy
and afraid of the crowd.
But he did pray every day
from morning 'til night.
By talking to God
his heart was made right.
In the silence of the church,
God heard ol' Dan's prayer.
The preacher heard nothing.
Why should he care?
As a tear rolled down
Ol' Farmer Dan's face,
He spoke to God in the lowest place.
#2: Oh God, I ain't much

like the rest of them.
I just hope You'll help me begin again.
'Cause the days ain't gettin' much
greener now.
And when it comes to feedin' the kids,
I just don't know how.
But Lord, You ain't never failed us
before.
You've always given us enough,
if not more.
Lord, we ain't special,
in fact, kind o' plain.
But Lord, we love You—
P.S. Send us some rain.
#1: After church they left
with grace and charm.
And Old Farmer Dan
went back to the farm.
The people went home
full of boasting and pride,
But Old Farmer Dan went home
justified.

The Net

#1: The kingdom of heaven is like a net
that was let down in the lake and caught
all kinds of fish.
#2: When it was full, the fisherman
pulled it up on the shore. *(Actors pantomime pulling a net out of the water with
much vocal effort.)*
#1: Then they sat down and collected
the good fish in baskets but threw the
bad away.
*(Actors pantomime the separation of fish
from waste.)*
#2: I hate seaweed. It always seems to
clog the net.
#1: Remember the Master said only
fish.
#2: Sure are a bunch of clams!

#1: Hey! Get that octopus out of here...
#2: Oh, great! A holy mackerel!
#1: Look, a large mouth bass!
#2: In salt water? That's impossible.
#1: Use your imagination—This is only
a play!
#2: Oops, I forgot.
#1: Why are the eels always on my side
of the net?
#2: A crab!
#1: There's another one.
#2: They sure are good to eat, but remember what the captain said—
#1, #2: Only fish.
#1: Too bad—
#2: This is how it will be at the end of
the age.
#1: The angels will come and separate
the wicked from the righteous.
#2: I hate sin. It always seems to clog
the net!
#1: Remember, the Master said only
the redeemed.
#2: Sure are a bunch of fornicators.
#1: Get that blasphemer out of here!
#2: Oh great, a Christian!
#1: Look, a short-winded pastor!
#2: That's impossible.
#1: Use your imagination—this is only
a play!
#2: Oops, I forgot!!
#1: Why are the gossipers always on my
side of the net?
#2: A church member!
#1: Hey! There's another one.
#2: They sure do look good but, but remember what the captain said—
#1, #2: Only Christians.
#1: Too bad.

64

The E.P.A.
by Karen Patitucci

(Bible study—James, relationships)
Scripture: James 3:9,10; Hebrews 3:13; 1
Thessalonians 5:11
Cast: Person, Agent
Props: Lab coat, imitation Geiger
counter, clipboard
(A very crabby person is changing channels on the television trying to find something to watch.)
PERSON: Reruns, news, cartoons, reruns, yuch . . . *(A knock at the door)* That's probably some idiot wanting some money for some dumb cause. *(Pretends to open door.)*
AGENT: Hello, I'm Susan with the E.P.A.
PERSON: I'm not interested. *(Shuts the door—agent knocks again—person opens the door.)* I'm *not* interested. *(Shuts the door.)*
AGENT: *(Yelling)* I don't want your money. *(Person opens the door.)*
PERSON: *(Immediate change of tone)* What do you want?
AGENT: Actually I'm here because some of your neighbors have registered a complaint with the Environmental Protection Agency which I represent.
PERSON: I'd be happy to sign a complaint. I think people who pollute the air should be prosecuted to the full extent of the law.
AGENT: *(Hesitating)* Well, the complaint is against you.
PERSON: Against me?
AGENT: The neighbors claim you've been polluting the air.
PERSON: Are you crazy? Do I look like someone who'd pollute the air? I don't own any toxic chemicals. I don't have an incinerator. I don't even smoke cigarettes.
AGENT: Twenty-five of your neighbors signed the complaint.
PERSON: Those idiots. *(Yells out the door.)* What kind of a dodo neighborhood did I move into? *(To Agent)* You'd think people could find something more important to complain about than me.
AGENT: They claim your curses are polluting the air.
PERSON: My curses? I don't swear. I stopped using four-letter words when I was in high school.
AGENT: There are other ways to curse people. Apparently *(Looking over the complaint)* some of the curses you often use include "jerk," "dumb," "ugly," "brat," "bore" . . .
PERSON: Those accusations are ridiculous. I want the name of your supervisor because I plan on making sure you lose your job because of this. Why, how'd they hire an imbecile like you?
AGENT: There you go again. Now you're cursing me.
PERSON: I still don't understand this "cursing" stuff.
AGENT: A curse means giving a person no respect, no value, no importance. The following words and phrases are all considered toxic to our environment: "idiotic," "ugly," "dumb," "stupid," "you're a nobody," "you'll never amount to anything" . . .
PERSON: I get the idea. I guess I'm going to have to learn to keep my mouth shut if I want to stop polluting the air.
AGENT: Or you can bless your

neighbors.

PERSON: Bless them?

AGENT: Yes. One of the ways you can do that is with words and phrases like: "That's great," "good job," "be careful," "I'd love to," "thank you" . . .

PERSON: Do you have a list of those?

AGENT: I sure do. *(Hands person list.)* Now, I'll be back in two weeks to check on the toxic levels and if there are no further complaints this petition will be destroyed and the fine waived.

PERSON: I'll work on it. I really will. *(Begins reading the list with difficulty.)* Good job, looks nice, great idea . . . I never even thought of some of these. *(Lights)*

Cheap Show
C. Exter Hardy III

(Discipleship Training,
Youth, discussion)

Setting: A car

Cast: Father, Teenage Daughter, Mother, Young Son (5–7 years old)

MOTHER: I can't believe that we didn't get out of church until *12:15* today. I guess the preacher doesn't realize that when he holds us over like that we end up at the end of the line for the buffet luncheon at the Holiday Inn.

FATHER: It wouldn't be so bad if the sermon was worth listening to. All he did was talk about tithing. I wish he would have talked more about God's love or grace or something that we need to hear.

DAUGHTER: He bores me to the max.

MOTHER: If you would listen to him you might get something out of it instead of flirting with Jimmy on the back row of the church.

FATHER: Yeah, I can't believe what you did during prayer!

MOTHER: Yes, I saw it too. The gall of you kissing him during the invitational prayer!

SON: I thought you were supposed to close your eyes when you pray? *(Silence by Mother and Father, Daughter snickers).*

FATHER: Did you smell the perfume that Mrs. Donaldson had on this morning?

MOTHER: Yes, it smelled like she was offering up a burnt offering!

FATHER: Who was the guy that gave the announcements this morning?

MOTHER: I don't know, but he sure did butcher them. He was so monotone I thought I would fall asleep before the sermon even started. Where did they dig him up anyway?

DAUGHTER: I don't know, but he didn't bother me as bad as Mrs. Peterson's solo. I thought my head would split if she didn't stop cracking all those high notes.

FATHER: I could have definitely done without her solo.

MOTHER: At least she wasn't as bad as the choir.

FATHER: I had never heard that arrangement before.

DAUGHTER: It wouldn't hurt my feelings if I never heard it again.

MOTHER: You know, I just didn't get much out of the service today.

SON: Well, I thought it was a pretty good show for just a dollar!

MONOLOGUES

That You May See
by Gail Blanton

(Church service, Bible study)
LEADER: *(Reads Rev. 3:15-18, NASB.)*
(Repeating a portion of the last verse) "I advise you to buy from Me . . . eyesalve to anoint your eyes, that you may see."
MAN: *(Enters, turns in a circle so that the audience gets a good look at him. He should be a stranger to them, or disguised that they do not recognize him. He is dressed in beggar's ragged clothes of the biblical period.)*
Hello there. How many of you have seen me before. You didn't see me by the door when you came in? I was right in the doorway, for heaven's sake! Sitting on the left, this pitiful look on my face, begging for money. You didn't see—oh never mind. I don't suppose you saw me last week either. Up in the balcony there. Ragged sweatsuit, sorta dirty, needed a haircut . . . no? I didn't think so. How about when I was waiting at the bus stop right here on this corner? Surely you noticed me—the one huddled up, shivering, the only one without a coat? No? I shouldn't wonder. Allow me to introduce myself. I am the ubiquitous unknown. Ubiquitous. That's a fancy word that just means appearing everywhere, seemingly at the same time. Ubiquitous. It rhymes with iniquitous. You should be able to remember that. I am the un-known that appear everywhere. And though you may not have seen me, I have most definitely seen you. I saw you when you went to the courthouse to pay your taxes and the policeman was taking me into the jail. That was a big parking lot we walked across. Didn't you see me? I saw you, too, when you ignored the little ringing bells and dashed into the Christmas rush. I saw you as I staggered up from my sleep the morning you came to work early. Did I use your parking space? Sorry. I was that latchkey kid last Tuesday too. Didn't you see how lonely I looked when you called your kids in for homemade cookies and milk? Oh yes, and I saw you hurrying to church that Sunday I was stranded on the highway with my four kids. I had on nice clothes that day and the car was fairly new. And you didn't see me? Well, like I said, I shouldn't wonder.

Do you know that I sat at the gate of a church—I mean we are talking big-time church here, as in *the* temple at Jerusalem. I sat there right in the gate, in this get-up, if you can believe it, for *30* years. Crippled. Unemployed. Finally one day two men named Peter and John saw me, I mean really saw me—at last. They prayed for me and I was healed. It was a wonderful day, but what took them so long?

Since then I've noticed that's what people like Peter and John and people like you have in common. People like you want to pray for people like me whenever they see us. That we'll be healed. And that's good. Nothing wrong with that. It's just that I'm gonna start praying for you to be healed too. I'm going to pray that you'll receive your sight . . . that you may see. *(As he exits)* Be seeing ya!

LEADER: "I advise you to buy from me . . . eyesalve to anoint your eyes, that you may see."

Say Glory
by Gail Blanton

(Church service, Bible study)

EARL: Once when I was about 13 my friend Ollie came home from church with me for lunch. It was just an ordinary Sunday dinner to us—talking about baseball cards and dove hunting—until Grandma came around to pour us more tea and she happened to be humming the hymn we had sung in church that morning. Ollie rolled his eyes sideways and kicked me under the table. The song was "O for a Thousand Tongues to Sing." "One's too many for some people," Ollie muttered. And his laugh escaped so suddenly that he almost choked on his chicken leg, and I spewed a shower of tea all over my plate. Grandma wanted to know what was so funny. Between fits of laughter we tried to tell her about Mrs. Logan's singing. See, some boy and girl that were "in love" had beaten us to the back row that morning. We didn't want to be anywhere near that, so we ended up sitting behind Mrs. Logan, more's the pity for our ears. I told Grandma a thousand tongues to sing like hers would close the place down. She was three notes slow and four notes sour, at full volume.

Grandma didn't think it was funny, and something about the way she set her pitcher down made us lose our sense of humor pretty quickly. I couldn't see why it was wrong to laugh at something so comical, so she made me look it up for myself. Psalm 29:9—"And in His temple everything says 'Glory!' " *(NASB)*. Then Grandma told us about something called sacrilege. We shrugged our shoulders and rolled our eyes some more, but Ollie ended up going home early and I couldn't get that verse out of my mind. All week long it would come to me at odd times, like a tune you can't get out of your head.

It could have been my conscience. See, the favorite pastime for us boys in church was looking through the songbook, saying the titles of hymns, and adding "in a pig's ear." I always knew it was wrong; that was what made it fun. "Hark! The Herald Angels Sing" in a pig's ear. "We're Marching to Zion" in a pig's ear. "Revive Us Again" in a pig's ear. Naturally, some were more sacrilegious than others. We were in serious trouble if everything in church was supposed to say "glory." We decided to check it out.

At a meeting of the Bonded Blood Brothers held in Ollie's treehouse we came up with a plan. We would say "glory" to ourselves after everything we heard in church—see if the gears meshed. We started listening to grown-ups first, sitting in a different pew every service. Talk about sacrilege!

"That rascal Marshall is hanging around me again," whispered the man in front of us. "I'm going to have to pay him off to get that paving contract."

"Glory," I said.

His wife whispered, "Look at that Katie. They've only been married two weeks and she's p.g."

"Double glory," sneered Ollie.

The experiment didn't last very long before we found out our church was far from Psalm 29. Now maybe you're not like that. Maybe you're very proper and say only proper things when you're in God's house. I'll even give you the parking lot. But I wonder if you remember God looks on the heart. What if you remembered every thought you've had since you came here today. How many can you follow with "glory"?

"I bet my roast is burning. Glory."

"I hate this old hymn. Glory."

"What a time I had last night! Glory."

"When is that preacher going to shut up? Glory!"

"Change it? Over my dead body. Glory!"

But we weren't talking about you, were we? We were talking about me. Well, while I was still trying to learn to be good on Sunday I became a Christian. And I found out that His temple saying "glory" is not just a church thing. It's an everyday thing. Everything I think or do or say—because my body is a temple— the temple of the Holy Spirit of God. Glory!!

Is God at Home?
by Gail Blanton

(Church service)

(Actor sits on platform with ministers at beginning of worship service. At a pre-arranged point he speaks, though he sits properly straight and still; only his eyes should move. These are his thoughts.)

I bet everybody is wondering why I'm sitting up here on the platform today. I can just hear them now: "He's not going to sing a solo, is he?" Goodness, I hope not. I told the pastor I had to make an announcement, but if he could read my thoughts right now . . . I'd like to tell him why I'm really up here. I'd like to tell everybody. Why, if they'd let me have a part in the service *(Comes forward and acts naturally now.)* I'd say:

When I was little I went to church with my Grandma. Every Sunday she would say, "Come on, Sonny, we're going to God's house." But the strange thing was, I never could find God there. I figured if it was His house He ought to be home sometime. I asked the preacher once if he was God, but he just laughed and said, "No, child, no." Once I saw a man with a beard. I had dropped my crayon and while I was down on the floor I slid on my back under two or three rows of seats, looking at the chewing gum stuck underneath. I looked over toward the window and there he sat. I chewed on my crayon and watched him for a while, but when he looked at me I scooted on back to Grandma. I found out it wasn't even God. It was Mr. Settlemeyer. Sometimes we had what they called the Lord's Supper, but I never saw

Him come and eat it. So, near the end of church-time the grownups would divide it. Everybody got just a taste. I didn't think it was enough to bother with, to tell the truth.

I decided God must stay in a secret room where children weren't allowed. When I was old enough to go to class by myself, I made up my mind to find God's room. I guess Grandma didn't realize how much it was bothering me, week after week looking for God at His house. I was ashamed to ask about it. After all, nobody else seemed to be looking for Him. Before class every Sunday I would check three or four different rooms. I would tiptoe down the empty hall as quietly as a cat, then pounce on the doorknob and jerk the door open. Before long I had searched the whole church and still hadn't found God. Scared a couple old ladies' classes out of their wits. Opened the door where the pastor's black waders were hanging over his boots and scared myself out of my wits. Went flying down the hall head-on into Deacon Redpath's stomach. He took me straight to Grandma. Embarrassed or not, I had to tell her what I had been doing. She must have seen then how important it was to me, because all she said was that we would have a long talk when we got home. And we did.

"Grandma," I said, "why is God never at His house?"

"Why, son, He's always there."

"Then where *is* He?"

"Why, he's inside the people who go there—most of them anyway. God is a spirit, so we can't see Him. But even if we could, He's so big and bright that we couldn't take it all in. So He took a little of His Spirit and put it in each one of His children. God planned it so that when we see another Christian we see just a little of what God is like. You look real close next Sunday and you'll see God smiling at you, God teaching your class, God shaking your hand, God singing to you."

I reminded Grandma about Mr. Kinlaw and asked her if that was God snoring every Sunday. She grinned and said, "No, He's just keeping the Spirit asleep in him right now. Some people push Him way down inside where He can't do much, and some people keep Him right up here close in their throats—soft as tears or loud as a hallelujah. You watch people, Son; you'll see just where God is."

And she was right. I learned to watch people closely. And the more I learned about God the more I saw Him in certain people. Persistently, no matter what happened, they always showed me God. But other people made me wonder if they weren't pretending all along.

Grandma died two months ago and naturally it started me reminiscing about all this. About Sundays with Grandma and a child's simple idea of where to find God. Lately I've realized that I kept coming to God's house, but somewhere along the road of habit and ritual I stopped looking for God. So I've had a longing to be up here where I can see Him—where I can watch your faces and search for God. I want to see if He is smiling or frowning today. Whether He looks troubled or at peace. Where He is pushed back or up close. Or whether He is here at all. (*His eyes scan the audience for a long moment—a pleasant look. He is not judgmental, merely seeking the truth. He returns to a seat in the sanctuary and the service continues as if nothing had ever happened.*)

Editor's Note: *This might be done effectively by two people—one doing the Grandmother—in Readers Theatre style.*

The Devil's Delight
by Robert Hughes

(Tithing, Giving)

(This will work best if the actor wears the traditional ridiculous devil's costume— red, long tail, horns, etc.—and is not seen until the moment he is to begin. Don't be afraid to be diabolical. Let the audience laugh . . . maybe they will then listen more carefully to the message!)

Welcome, devils, to this week's temptation teleconference. I understand some of you lesser darks have been complaining about having to watch this "boring TV garbage." Let me remind you that while complaints, backbiting, and rebellion are generally encouraged, by direct order from below, ANY devil who fails to give heed to the lessons we discuss will be weeping and gnashing his teeth! I HOPE I make myself clear? As to television being boring, just remember—it HAS been one of our finest tools of temptation in recent years.

Now to the content of today's lecture, entitled "Furthering Fiscal Sin." First, what is this delicious morsel we call fiscal sin? Fiscal sin is the misuse of money, any money, which might be used by these foolish mortals to healthier, so-called "better" ends. Of course, we want to encourage fiscal sin as much as possible—waste, greed, bribery, gambling, opulence—all of these are among our finest corruptions of (*Bitterly, pointing upwards*) His creation. But I've been asked to make a special point today of dealing with an issue horribly threatening to ALL devils. I mean, of course, the contribution to (*With disgust*) church stewardship campaigns. The more successful these campaigns are, the more our freedom to tempt, lie, confuse, distort, and destroy human lives will be limited!

Therefore, I'm authorized to command you to give special attention to churches in your region who are talking about giving. We MUST do SOMETHING to confuse these fools into NOT GIVING! (*Chuckles*) Fortunately, we have a great many tools at our disposal—perfected during CENTURIES of successful operations! (*Thoughtfully*) I remember one of my finest programs was the sale of indulgences. (*Frowning*) If only that pain, Martin Luther, hadn't interfered with his—but I digress. I am here to give you several quick, time-tested temptations to untrack the most (*With disgust*) faithful believer:

First—Make them feel GUILTY about how much they're currently NOT giving. Now, I realize guilt doesn't seem to have the impact with our OWN people that it once did, those wonderful captives of ours still deliciously IN their SINS—but with these church types condemnation is still QUITE successful. So make them feel very, VERY guilty. That will make them angry! Then, they'll either refuse to give at all—to prove their independence, you see—or else they'll give grudgingly—and then turn around and criticize their fellow church member who gives less than they. Oh I know, if they give at all it's no victory for us, but with a little work you can MAYBE turn them into a Pharisee—which will help keep other prospective believers away!

Second—Make them overspend! Then they'll be so busy paying off their credit card debts they'll not have money to *(Ulp!)* tithe. Get them overextended, then whisper in their ears 'You can make up for this NEXT month . . .' *(Chuckles)* Of course, they never WILL . . . And if you get them far enough in the hole they may become so embarrassed they never come to church again!

A third—Make them believe it's their OWN money they're putting into the plate and not *(Pointing upward, with disgust)* HIS. Then when they get upset over something the church does or doesn't do, they can stand up self-righteously in business meeting and say "I don't give my money to support . . ." whatever it is they're angry about. Work this right, and they'll stop giving entirely! Work it REALLY well, and they'll feel JUSTIFII D in not supporting their own church or denomination! Oh, how the rafters below ring with laughter when THAT happens!

Fourth—Make them believe giving is an investment! This is one of our most marvelous scams—convince the fools that they can get a better return on their tithing dollar than they can on a Certificate of Deposit. Of course, you have to be careful with this—*(Pointing up, with disgust)* He has been known to *(Bitterly)* open up the windows of—that place and pour out blessings! Still, there are enough times that He doesn't that we can work on the credibility of that argument—the fools tithe, then get themselves in debt, then blame HIM! Now THAT would be a find piece of devilry, to be sure!

Number five—Make them focus on the opulence of their buildings and grounds, instead of on the so-called "needs" of those who already belong to us! They'll spend all their energy—AND money!—to make themselves comfortable inside their own churches—or to look really SPIFFY on the softball diamond—or to be able to point with succulent pride to their edifice and say "We have the prettiest church in this town!" ENCOURAGE exorbitant expenditures on such inessentials all you can. Then we'll be left alone to do our worst!

These are only five, but oh devils, there are THOUSANDS of ways to use money to entrap, encumber, distract, confuse, and otherwise incapacitate those who belong to *(With disgust)* HIM . . . ! *(Threatening)* And you'd better be USING them all right now! For at this very moment in *(Bitterly)* churches around the world, these fools are contributing funds designated to BRING DOWN OUR HIGHLY REPULSIVE EMPEROR! And others are USING those funds against us, in lands we've OWNED for centuries! If these monies are allowed to fall into the wrong hands, temptations could be diminished, sin could be—perish the thought—overcome, and our captives, upon whom we feed, be freed from darkness into (*Gag!*) light!

Worst of all, what happens when these (*Ulp!*) believers begin to cooperate TO-GETHER, begin to budget vast sums of money in a withering onslaught against us! We must DESTROY such a cooperative program! Stifle it! Cut it off at the roots! Otherwise—knowing (*With disgust*) Him—it will mean our more hasty downfall!

Heed my warning, fellow devils! For if you don't, and He wins the world—it will be YOU and ME our dark ruler will be roasting and eating!

The Madman of the Garden
by Gerald Morris

(Church service)

(*A young man, standing alone*)

Sometimes I see things. I don't mean I see the future or anything, but sometimes I see what people are thinking. You might think it's a gift. It's not. It's a curse.

You see, people can see that I'm different, and they avoid me. And until five years ago, I avoided them, too. I could see what meanness was in their minds, and I wanted nothing to do with them. But then, as I said, five years ago something happened.

My mother and I lived in Jerusalem. It happened there. One Passover she invited a man to have Passover dinner in our upstairs room. It was Jesus of Nazareth My sister and I had to help serve the meal and so I was there.

I have never known a man like that man. And I have never felt such anguish as I felt when I was near Him. It was all around Him. I remember when He and His friends sat down that He sat down slowly, as if He had been carrying a dead weight all day. His friends began chattering away about the sights they had seen that day. Most of them were from the country and seldom came to Jerusalem. And all this time I began to feel something coming from Jesus. I moved closer to find out what it was.

How can I describe it? His mind was black and heavy like pitch. Everything I saw then was shaded with blackness. He looked down once at His hands, and I swear I saw blood dripping from them. I know I saw it, but the next moment he looked away, and the blood was gone. I was terrified. I had seen into the minds of people in grief before, but never had I seen such grief as this. His mind boiled with a swirling, confused hell of darkness.

And the worst part of it was that His friends were so blind. I wanted to scream at them to look at Jesus, but couldn't make any noise. On my right, two of His friends were talking about knives, arguing about which one of them had the best dagger. "But the blade, that's all that's important on a knife." "Without the point the dagger is useless. It's all in the point." On the other side of the room—I remember this clearly—someone was thinking about my sister and wondering if she was married. To my left was a man who was mentally counting his money. (*Pause*) He had 30 pieces of silver.

(*He begins talking louder, more quickly, gradually approaching hysteria.*)

And all this while, Jesus was in more

agony that I had ever seen. We served the bread and then . . . Jesus broke it. I'll never forget the pain again. For a moment I saw Him naked, slashed, and bleeding. And then He spoke. He said, "This is My body which is broken for you. Eat it, and remember Me when I am gone." I wanted to scream. But no one even noticed that He had said anything out of the ordinary. Everyone was thinking about his food—except for the man across the room—he was wondering how to get my sister's attention.

And then we served the wine. It was blood. I could have sworn it was blood. There was blood everywhere. It dripped from the walls and the ceiling. We were all spattered with it, and we all just kept talking happily. I looked into Jesus' face, and I saw that He was looking into mine. And then suddenly His whole face became a mask of blood. I threw down the pitcher I was holding and backed into a corner. I found my voice and I screamed and screamed, "Blood! It's blood! Don't drink it, Jesus!"

(*Wildly*) Then my mother grabbed me. She was crying. I was crying too. She took me downstairs and undressed me and put in my bed in my room. I think I was still screaming when she shut the door.

(*He pauses, then continues more collectedly.*)

After a while I stopped screaming, and I began to think. I began to get angrier at Jesus' friends—thinking about money, and women, and knives while their master was suffering so much. I wanted to go tell them what He had been feeling while they were busying themselves with their little trivial concerns.

I guess I was still hysterical because I didn't even think to put on clothes. I ran upstairs naked. And they were gone.

Mother had seen me, and she came to me while I stood there confused. She wrapped me in a sheet. She was trying to comfort me, but she didn't understand. I had to go to Jesus' friends to tell them that Jesus needed them. I ran downstairs, out into the street, and then off to the town. I didn't know where I was going or where Jesus was likely to be; I just ran. I must have run for two hours. Finally, just outside of town, In a garden, I felt I was near. Then I saw Jesus. He was kneeling alone, praying. His friends were . . . asleep. They had no idea what their leader was enduring.

In Jesus' mind I saw something different, though. At the table His mind had been dark. Now it was light. I could see faces, hundreds of faces, going in and out of His thoughts. I saw His friends, some people I didn't know, then just face after face. I saw my face there too. I realized suddenly that these were the people that He loved, all the people that He knew, and He loved them all.

All of a sudden, I didn't want to scream at His sleeping friends; I wasn't angry at all. I wished I could tell them what I had seen, but I didn't want to do it in rebuke; I wanted to tell them just to show that Jesus had loved them. (*Pause*)

The soldiers came that night to take Him away, but I don't think it made any difference to me—or to Jesus. I think we both knew that the real battle had been won when the blackness of fear left Him and love took over.

Sometimes I used to see things. I don't know why, but sometimes I did. I used to think it a curse. You see, people sometimes avoided me because they could see I was a little different from the rest of the world. I used to avoid them, too, when I would see how trivial and mean their minds were, but I don't any more. How can I avoid them? I love them.

The Blind Man
by John Lee Welton

(Church service)
(The man comes on stage, feeling his way. When he reaches center, he stops, and holding out his hand, calls for alms.)

Alms . . . Alms. Alms . . . *(He faces the audience.)* All I had to do was listen— and to ask. It was as simple as that. But you see—I was afraid. Afraid that what I had heard about Him was just a lie. Afraid to be disappointed. Afraid to be something I had never been before.

You see, my world, as bad as it was, was familiar to me. Even though I hated it, there was a kind of comfort in my familiar darkness. The world described to me by others was a foreign land—a place filled with strange sensations called light and color—just words that meant nothing to me.

The only real comfort I found was in my friend, who, like myself, had been blind since childhood. Together we shared our pain. But where I feared what that other world might be like, he seemed to imagine it as a place of miracles. I listened to his dreams, but silently I scoffed at his foolishness.

But then one day he came to me filled with uncontrollable excitement. He said he had heard this man—a prophet of some kind—tell of a place where there would be no more pain, where the lame could walk and the blind could see.

"You're a fool," I told him. "Chase after this merchant of dreams if you want, but you won't find me dancing to the song of this singer of lies."

"Come with me and hear Him speak," my friend pleaded. But I shoved him aside and stumbled back here to the safety of my little corner near the temple, where I beg for alms from the worshipers passing by.

It was many days before I heard the voice of my friend again. When he called my name there was a strange sound in his throat—a sound of great pain. He took my face in his hands and turned it up toward his own as he stood there above me. As he whispered my name again, I felt drops of warm water fall on my face.

"My friend," I said as I reached up to him, "you're weeping!"

"Yes," he said quietly. "I weep from a great hurt."

Suddenly I knew what had happened. *(Angrily)* He had gone to this prophet with His dreams of the other world, and now he was returning to me, empty and disappointed as I knew he would. My heart ached for him and I wanted to hold him close and pull his darkness into mine, giving him the little strength that comes from shared sorrow. "I'm sorry, my old friend," I said as I rose and took him in my arms. "I'm sorry you didn't find your dream."

He slowly held me away and a great

75

sob shuddered through him. "No, my friend," he said. "You don't understand. I had to come back here. I had to *see* you, even though I had to close my eyes to find my way here. I weep not for myself, but for you my friend, who sits in darkness." And then he took my hands from his arms and backed slowly away to his new world, the world I had feared and longed for, and cannot see—because I would not hear.

(Reaching out to the audience.) Alms. Alms. Won't you help the blind? Alms.

Mary
by Eddie Morgan

(Church service, Easter,
Bible study)

I was so excited about His coming. Every few minutes I would run from the house and look up the street to see if He was in sight. Martha, my sister would get *so* angry.

"Will you get back in here and help me finish cooking?"

So back and forth I would go, looking for Jesus and helping Martha. I must have been worthless in the kitchen. Martha looked over at me and shouted...

"If you are going to mess everything up, just leave! Go on out there and wait."

I was hoping she would say that. Off I went. I ran to the road and stood just so I could see around the curve.

He's coming! I see Him. Martha, He's coming! I lost all my words. I had this beautiful speech planned, but what came out of my mouth? "Nice day isn't it, think we will ever get rain, you are shorter than I thought." I felt so stupid. He just smiled, touched my hand and said "Good afternoon, Mary."

We were all together, Jesus, His disciples, Martha, Lazarus, and me.

His words were so powerful. I was glued to my chair as He shared with us. He taught us about prayer, forgiveness, peace, and hope. He understood my feelings. Martha, on the other hand, didn't seem to care. All she wanted to do was get lunch cooked and make everything j-u-s-t right.

When He left I felt sad, but not empty, for He assured me that He would see us again.

A few months later, our little brother, Lazarus, became very sick. I prayed every day for his health, but the more I prayed, the sicker he became. I knew his only hope was Jesus. We sent out messengers, looking, but Jesus was no where to be found. Then came word that He was just over in the next town. I sent word for Him to please come now! We waited. Jesus never came. Lazarus died.

I was angry, hurt, and confused. How could Jesus let my brother die? Two days later I was outside, alone with my grief, when I saw Him coming up the road. Still angry, I ran inside. Martha met Jesus at the door. I could hear them talking. Then I heard Jesus ask for me. I stormed out ready to give Him a piece of my mind. But as I looked up I could see that Jesus, too, was crying.

Embarrassed about my doubts and ashamed of my hate, I ran to His outstretched arms. He comforted me and asked to see Lazarus. "Lord he has been dead for four days, I don't think . . ."

But He insisted. We went to the tomb. Jesus had His disciples move the stone away from the entrance. No sooner had Jesus entered than He was coming back out—alone.

But then I saw Him smiling as He said, "Come Lazarus, come out among the living."

There he was, Lazarus! Still bound by his burial clothes, but alive! We returned home and celebrated and talked well into the next morning. I so wanted Jesus to know of my thanks and devotion. The only thing I could think to do was wash His feet in oil. Both Martha and Judas thought I was being extravagant. I didn't care. Jesus knew I was just being thankful.

After everyone else had gone to bed, Jesus and I sat outside and talked until sunup. He reassured me, and helped me to grow. The more we talked the more I understood myself and understood His purpose.

Except for one thing. As we watched the sun rise that morning He began to talk to me about His death. "Lord You are the Son of God. You cannot die."

"I can and I must," He said. "Mary remember what I told you, 'I am the resurrection and the life. Whoever believes in Me will live, even though he dies; and whoever lives and believes in Me will never die' *(John 11:25, NIV)*. I must be the life and resurrection not just for Lazarus, but for everyone. Mary My time is short, I must soon go."

But Lord, "What will happen to us?" Then He replied softly, "so as the sun is rising on this day, so too will the Son of Man rise again and you will never be alone."

He got up, dusted Himself off, reached down to help me and gave me an *enormous* hug. And without saying a word, He smiled, wiped a tear from my eye, then wiped away His own tears, turned, and left.

As the sun rose higher in the sky, I was reminded of what He had said . . .

"So too will the Son of Man rise again and you will never be alone."

I called out one last time as He was leaving, "Will I see you for Passover?" No reply.

Emotions flooded my soul. Frightened, confused, yet loved and at peace. I watched Him until He disappeared from sight. But He would never disappear from my heart. He *was* right. You never have to walk alone.

(Lights fade, Mary exits.)

Martha, The Busy Hostess
by John Lee Welton

(Church service, Easter,
Bible study)

I don't know which I felt the most—anger or hurt. It wasn't like me, but I went out and cried, my tears dropping into the water as I leaned on the stone wall surrounding the well.

I had tried my best, my very best, to honor Him. I had stayed up half the night preparing food while my sister, Mary, slept soundly.

"Why are you so grumpy this morning," she asked when she finally got out of bed.

All I did was ask her if she could at least put the bread dough in the oven.

She never could see what work had to be done without my telling her.

"In a minute," she replied between yawns.

She piddled around, washing her face, combing her long black hair, fixing it just so. And all the while I hurried about trying to get the roast lamb ready.

"Never mind," I snapped. "I'll put the dough in."

"I'll be right there," she chirped happily. "I want to look well when we see Jesus."

"Look well, indeed," I mumbled to myself, seeing my own flour-covered face reflected in the bowl of wash water. My hair hung in sweaty strands, plastered there by the heat from the cooking fire.

I paused for a moment to really look at myself. I had never been pretty. Mary was the pretty one in our family—but I was the one everyone could depend on. "Good old Martha always took care of everybody."

Even when Lazarus was so sick, all Mary could do was walk the floor, wringing her hands, and praying. And when he died, she shut herself up in her room and cried while I had to greet the mourners. When I heard that Jesus was finally coming, I was the one who hurried to tell Him that Lazarus had already died. But Jesus asked me to go back and get Mary. Even though I had nursed Lazarus, even though I had been the one who had sent for Jesus, He still wanted to see Mary.

I guess I could understand that, she needed His strength, too. But what I really couldn't understand was why He had rebuked me later.

It was after He had given Lazarus back his life. A dinner was given in Jesus' honor at the house of Simon the leper. Well, he wasn't a leper any more—Jesus had cured him—but we had called him that for so long it was hard not to think of him as Simon the leper.

Of course the women weren't invited to eat with the men, but we did have the privilege of serving the food. Fortunately not everybody ate—some had just crowded in to gape at my brother and Simon—and at the miracle worker who had given them back their lives. But even then I had to keep on the run just to feed the invited guests. Of course Mary had come along on the pretense of helping me serve, but instead she just stood around, listening to every word Jesus said. She even got so bold she sat down near Him, listening to Him wide-eyed like a child. There she sat, doing nothing to help. I guess I shouldn't have said anything, but when I bumped into one of the onlookers and spilled a whole pitcher of wine, my anger just went all over me!

"Master," I blurted out, interrupting what He was saying. "Will you please tell my sister to help me serve the guests—at least until after everyone has had a chance to eat?"

Jesus sat for a moment, just looking from Mary to me. Then very slowly and quietly He said, "Martha, dear friend, you are so upset over all these details! There is really only one thing worth being concerned about. Mary has discovered it—and I won't take it away from her!' " (Luke 10:41-42, TLB)

In front of all those people, Jesus said that Mary's sitting there doing nothing was more important than all the work I had done! I felt my face flush. I picked up the water jug and hurried out of the room on the pretense of going to the well for more water. But the only water that poured forth was the angry tears streaming down my face. And to make things worse, when I went back in, the whole place smelled with the sweet odor of perfume. Mary had brought an expensive oil and had poured it on Jesus' feet, and now she was wiping them with her hair! It wasn't enough that she be so bold as to sit as His feet, but now she had tried to use this flattery to gain His attention! Even one of the disciples chastised her for what she had done. But Jesus put His hand on Mary's head and said something about her anointing Him for His burial. *What a morbid thing to say, I thought!*

It wasn't until after He had died that I finally understood what Jesus had meant. Somehow He knew of His own death at the hands of the Roman soldiers. And as we were washing His body, cleansing it for the burial cloths, it came to me that Mary seemed to have more strength than I had ever seen in her. It was as if she had been prepared for this task—prepared by her actions that evening at the dinner. Always before she had stood back and waited for me to take charge, but now she boldly went about the heartrending business of preparing His body for burial.

As I watched her work, I suddenly realized what Jesus had meant when He said that she was providing what was needed. The greatest gift she could give was herself, giving Him her undivided attention, sharing her needs, and her love with Him. And He was giving her what she needed—the strength to face the task before both of them—to face His death on the cross.

And as I watched her work, something else became clear to me. God had already blessed *me* with a wonderful gift—with the strength and deep desire to support others less strong than myself. Mary and Lazarus had always needed me to be strong for them, to be in charge where they couldn't. That was my gift and my mission—to care for others. And just as that was my mission and my need, so Mary needed to share with others—to share herself, to listen to them, to question, to entice others to open their minds and their hearts to her.

Mary stopped her work for a moment to wipe away the tears, so she could see to wrap the winding sheet about the body of the one we both loved so much.

I touched her shoulder and when she turned to me, I said, "What can I do to help?" I waited for *her* to tell *me* how I could best serve. With a gentle smile she took something from her robe, then slowly held out the jar of sweet smelling oil. I took it from her, and *I* lovingly, tenderly, anointed His nail-pierced feet.

Mary Magdalene
by Lisa Currie

(Church service)

When I was a little girl, all the boys would tease me because my hair was so short. They would say that I looked like a little boy. They said I was ugly.

I would cry for hours; I hated those little boys. But mama would sit me in her lap and tell me that I was the prettiest girl in all of Magdala. It wasn't much help though. Magdala was only a small village and there weren't many girls my age anyway.

How I hated those little boys. And I made a promise to myself that I would let my hair grow long, and it would be beautiful, and then the little boys wouldn't tease me anymore.

Well I kept my promise. My hair grew long and it was beautiful and instead of teasing me, they used me. They used my hair. They used my hair to wrap themselves in, to keep them warm on cold nights, to hide from their nagging wives. They didn't tease me anymore. They needed me now. Needed me to get away from their wives who had grown fat from having too many children.

Now—it was the women who teased me. The women who were too ashamed of me, too ashamed of themselves. Too ashamed of their fat bodies that their husbands didn't want anymore.

They were too ashamed to show their bodies to more than one man.

The *women* teased me now, but I didn't go home and cry like I did when I was a little girl. No, I was proud. I walked through the streets and through the market as proud as any woman. *I* wasn't fat from too many children and I wasn't ashamed to show my body to more than one man.

But inside—I hurt—because I knew every man in Magdala knew who I was; every man in Capernaum knew who I was, *what* I was. But I, I was too proud.

Then the news spread of this man from Nazareth. He was a prophet they said. Prophet, eh? I had had many prophets in my house; they weren't prophets at all, just angry men with a loud voice and nothing better to do.

I was going to see just how much of a prophet this man was! One day I saw Him in a crowd, but He didn't see me. The next time I saw Him, in Capernaum, I made sure He saw me: I got right down in front of Him and . . . He just *looked* at me. He looked at me with compassion, not lust or love, but compassion. He knew me. He knew everything about me. He knew me better than I knew myself.

I couldn't stay. I couldn't stand in front of those piercing eyes; I had to run, to leave, to hide. For the first time since I was a little girl I was ashamed—in front of Him, a man. All the childhood feelings of hatred and anger and shame were back. I was angry at all those men who had dirtied my hair.

After this meeting, my thoughts were consumed with this Jesus of Nazareth. I *wanted* to be near Him, to touch Him. I wanted Him to tell me that I was beautiful again, and to make my hair clean again.

I found out that He was going to be at a Pharisee's house for dinner. Should *I* dare go in there? They all knew me well, but were ashamed to admit it. They knew me better than they knew their own wives.

The minute the crowd saw me they parted like flies . . . they dare not be touched by such an unclean woman—a harlot.

I went in and He was sitting there and again, He just looked at me. Just *looked*. But at that moment, I knew that I was clean. My hair was beautiful again.

I wanted so much to tell Him, to show Him, but I had no words—only tears, tears that I poured over His beautiful feet . . . the feet of a beautiful man that set me free. He made my hair clean again. And so I gave it to him—wiping my tears from His feet.

Then I stood and stared at this man and He said to me: "Go and sin no more." Well He didn't even have to tell me that! My hair was clean and there was no way that I was ever going to let it get dirty again.

I left there free at last, clean at last— and no one dared to tease me anymore, because my hair was clean.

The Two Marys
by Gerald Morris

(Adult groups)
(*A middle-aged woman alone on stage*)

I thought it such a great honor at first. Jesus of Nazareth was going to eat the Passover meal in my home. I spent—oh, I must have spent eight or nine hours cleaning the upstairs room. We never use it, so it was a bit of a mess, with dust everywhere and all of John Mark's old toys just tossed up there on the floor.

But of course it was worth it. Not every home has a famous man come eat there, especially on a feast day. I could already see what that little old woman at the end of the street would look like when she found out. She who was so proud of the new clothes she had made last Passover. I tried not to be spiteful about it, but I did enjoy imagining what her reaction would be when she found out that Jesus of Nazareth ate Passover with me.

But of course my joy was dampened a bit when I saw Jesus. He didn't look like a celebrity, in spite of the crowds around Him. I had had the whole family put on their best clothes to welcome Him, and we looked so much nicer than He did that I was almost sorry for Him. And His friends. I'd heard that he had 10 or 12 followers who went everywhere with Him, so I'd set 13 places. There must have been 25 who followed Him upstairs, without so much as a by-your-leave. What could I do? And then—I look back at this and laugh now—He asked if I had a foot basin. Well, of course my first thought was, *I forgot to wash their feet. Of all the silly things to forget* . . . and so on. I got all flustered inside and ran and got it myself, then called my servant to come wash their feet—but of course that wasn't what He wanted. He took the basin and began washing all His friends' feet. Well, He wasn't your typical dinner guest.

But—here's the part that really shook me—then He called for me to come to Him. Or at least He called my name, "Mary." So of course, model hostess that I am, I ran to see what He wanted— and embarrassed myself again, naturally. He was calling someone else with the same name. It wouldn't have been so bad—I mean that happens to everybody sometime—but the Mary he was calling was . . . a harlot.

I hadn't even seen her come in—which was just as well, I suppose, since I would have told her to stay out and embarrassed myself again—and I just stood and stared while Jesus of Nazareth talked to this woman. My mouth dropped open, my eyes widened, the whole bit—and of course someone noticed, and pretty soon everyone noticed and was laughing at me, or almost everyone.

Jesus wept.

That night, after the dinner, the priests came and took Him away, and I woke up the next morning to hear the news all over the city that Jesus was arrested.

And tried.

And condemned, all in the same day.

We crowded in the streets that afternoon, to see the spectacle—Jesus of Nazareth carrying a cross to Golgotha, to be crucified. And once I got into the crowd, there was no turning back—or turning to one side—or even stopping. I was carried along toward Golgotha whether I wanted to go or not, and right next to me, carried along just like I was, was the harlot. I remember thinking, *Oh, great. The two Marys.* It took us hours to get to the hill where He was to be put up, everything moved so slowly. We never even saw Him until we got there; the crowd was just too thick.

And then there He was, already up on the cross. I couldn't believe it; it had happened so fast. I stood there for a long time—I don't know how long—completely unaware that there was anything in the world except me and the dying man on the cross. I was completely wrapped up in my own sorrows, in myself. Then I heard Jesus say, "Father forgive them. They don't understand." What kind of man was this? A man who forgives His murderers? I stood and stared. Finally I woke up and looked around. I guess I'd been there for a long time; the crowd was almost all gone. I hadn't even noticed the other people leaving. Now there were only a handful left on the hill: a few of His friends, His mother, me, and the other Mary.

I couldn't keep my eyes off her. In the crowd she had been mauled by those who knew she was a harlot. The men who had wanted her body but had been afraid of what people would say had found their chance in the anonymous crowd, and they had felt her body and ripped her clothes. She was almost naked up there on that barren hill, right underneath Jesus. At first I thought she was bleeding, but then I realized that some of Jesus' blood had dripped on her bare back.

You've got to imagine her. She was shaking with great big gasping sobs, and her face—dusty from the crowd—was streaked with mud from her tears. But most of all, I realized she wasn't crying because of the way she had been manhandled. She was crying because her Lord was dying above her. There she knelt, naked as a baby, most of her makeup rubbed off by the crowd or washed off by her own tears, and . . . she was just a child! She looked like a little girl—an orphan. I didn't even think about what I was doing. I went to her and held her at my breast. And I cried with her, the poor child. We knelt there at the foot of God Himself, the mother and the harlot, and cried together. We were all crying, or almost all.

Jesus smiled.

EGO: Edging God Out
by Tonna Davis

(Discussion)

Characters: 2 females, 1 male, 2 either

NARRATOR: (*Center stage*) EGO means *E*dging *G*od *O*ut. (*Freeze with head down.*)

LADY: Well, finally! The nominating committee finally asked me to teach a Sunday School class. From what I heard, the last teacher they had was . . . well . . . I think I could certainly do a better job. Of course, I'm a very busy person, but I'll set aside time on Saturday to study and I'll have a last minute review Sunday morning on the way to church. I believe in being prepared to teach *my* class. (*Freeze*)

MAN: That phone call was from the chairman of the deacons. They want me to be considered for ordination! Imagine! I'll be able to sit in on all those "secret" meetings and tell the church what needs to be done. *I* have some good ideas on how to better manage our budget. Maybe I'll be considered for treasurer. Then, we'll see things happen around here because *I* am a successful businessman and *I'll* use *my* brain for business to instruct the church. (*Freeze*)

YOUTH: My Youth Minister chose me to be the leader of our Backyard Bible Club. He can recognize genuine leadership when he sees it! Besides, *I'm* more spiritual and older than most of the other youth. *I* can handle responsibility and authority. Just wait until our next youth meeting! Won't those youth be surprised when *I* start giving the orders. (*Freeze*)

LADY: The present president of the WMU just called me and asked me to consider being president of WMU next year. Why doesn't someone ask me to do something really important? (*Freeze*)

NARRATOR: (*Looks at audience.*) EGO means Edging *God* Out.

READERS THEATRE AND CHORAL READING

Remembering Jesus
by James C. Evans

(Adapted for Readers Theatre
by John Lee Welton)
(Lord's Supper meditation
or Easter)

Characters: 3 males, 2 females, 1 extra

(Simple staging and costuming is all that is required to make a very meaningful Lord's Supper meditation or Easter outreach event.)

NARRATOR: The scene is a dimly candlelit room in the home of Lazarus of Bethany. It is a late summer evening in the year 33 A.D. The near silence of the room and the dimness of the light disguise the fact that the room is filled with people, almost 50-strong. A man with head bowed prays softly at the front of the room—chanting, really, more than speaking, and when he pauses, every eye turns to him.

JAMES: I bid you peace in the name of our Lord

ALL: Peace to you, James.

JAMES: Our "Lord Jesus in the night in which He was betrayed took bread; and when He had given thanks, He broke it, and said [to His disciples], 'This is My body, which is for you; do this in remembrance of Me'" *(1 Cor. 11:23-24, NASB).*

NARRATOR: And with that, James, the brother of Jesus, took a loaf of unleavened bread and broke it and passed it among the believers.

JAMES: So do we remember the Lord Jesus.

ALL: In remembrance of the Lord Jesus.

NARRATOR: James' eyes teared as he went on.

JAMES: Jesus . . . His name sounds so different to my ears now that I truly know Him. All those years growing up, knowing Him only as an older brother. We all knew He was not like us, and yet . . . and yet we did not believe . . . we could not believe. It was not until He appeared to me alive—after I had seen Him crucified—that I believed, and to this very day I know that Jesus is Lord.

THOMAS: I know unbelief, and how it can become belief!

NARRATOR: The strong voice of Thomas startled the group.

THOMAS: I was with Him for three years, every day listening to Him, learning faith from Him. I remember the day we learned of Lazarus' death. Jesus said He would go to Bethany, but many warned Him of the danger. But I said to the others "Let us go with Him that we may die with Him." I thought of those words many times after I deserted Him in the garden that night . . . that I thought I would die for Him. *(Pauses)* The shame of my failure caused me to be absent from the others when He appeared alive to them. I wanted to believe their report . . . but I could not. His death was too real to me. I wanted the proof of His resurrection to be just as real. I can see Him even now saying, "Thomas, 'reach here your finger, and see My hands; and reach here your hand, and put it into My side; and be not unbelieving, but believing'" *(John 20:27, NASB)*. . . . When I remember Jesus, I remember Him as the one who turned unbelieving hearts into believing hearts.

RACHEL: I remember Jesus as one who knows what is in our hearts.

NARRATOR: She spoke with a voice as lovely as her dark eyes.

RACHEL: I am Rachel, of Samaria. I shall never forget the day my heart became opened to Him. When we met, I saw only a Jew, and a man, neither of which I trusted. But when He spoke to me, it was as though He looked right through me, to my very heart. It mattered not how I sought to deceive Him or to trap Him into useless debate. He cut through all my defenses and exposed my heart. Yet He did not condemn me, rather He seemed to draw me to His . . . His love. He made me blush . . . I had not blushed in years. In my shame and fear, I spoke of the Messiah, hoping that He would scold me for speaking of "their" Messiah. I still can see His eyes as He said, "I am He." That was the first time I ever really knew what love was. Yes, I remember Jesus, I remember Him as the one who knows our hearts.

NARRATOR: Rachel spoke these last thoughts with eyes lowered, and when she looked up, what she saw caused her to gasp. Following her gaze, the others now saw what had taken her breath. There in the doorway stood the towering figure of a Roman soldier. His eyes scanned the room of silent believers, until finally he broke the silence with a voice that commanded their attention.

SOLDIER: You are followers of the Galilean? Of Jesus of Nazareth?

NARRATOR: It was not so much a question as it was a command to confess. James spoke for them all.

JAMES: We are followers of Jesus Christ, the Son of God. What do you seek?

SOLDIER: I seek you! It was told to me that His followers met in Bethany. I came . . . to warn you that others will come to arrest you all. You must not remain here long.

JAMES: Why do you warn us?

SOLDIER: I have listened to you speak of remembering Jesus. I, too, remember Him. I was assigned to the guard in Capernaum, where I heard Him teach and saw Him heal the sick. When a servant of mine became ill, I sought Him out and asked of Him healing for my servant. He not only healed my servant, but He spoke of my faith. "'Go your way,'" He said to me. "'Let it be done to you as you have believed'" *(Matt. 8:13, NASB)*. I thought He was referring to my servant, because he was healed that very hour. Later I realized He had meant more . . . that something was new inside me because I had believed.

I heard little of Him after that, until "that day." I had been sent to Jerusalem to keep the guard over crucifixions there. That day, I was ordered to crucify one called "Jesus, King of the Jews." As I watched Him die, somehow I realized who He was, and when He died, something inside me died too.

NARRATOR: From the front, a beautiful, middle-aged woman leaned her face toward the soldier.

MARY: *(Softly)* Centurion, I was there. As our Lord died, I heard it, but I did not know who said it. " 'Truly this was the Son of God,' " *(Matt. 27:54, NASB)* someone said. It was you, wasn't it?

SOLDIER: It was I, and I have said it to myself a thousand times since. When I heard that He had risen, I came to verify it for myself.

MARY: He is risen, and we have seen Him.

SOLDIER: Then I may go in peace, for I now know with my mind what my heart has known since the day I saw the empty tomb. Thank you, thank you all.

NARRATOR: With that, he turned to leave.

MARY: Centurion, my Son was right, you have great faith.

NARRATOR: The centurion paused as Mary's words penetrated him.

MARY: Take care, that you may keep your life, and have many days to remember Him.

NARRATOR: The centurion's footsteps still sounded in the night air as Lazarus' voice rang out.

LAZARUS: I remember Jesus every day I am alive, for I have known death and life again. It seems only yesterday that I lay on my deathbed. My sisters, Mary and Martha, sat by my side and wept. "I have sent for Jesus," Mary said. And I had sudden hope. Martha went to prepare for His arrival, while Mary and I prayed He would arrive before it was too late. I remember closing my eyes and saying "Abba, Father" and, what seemed like the next moment I heard Jesus calling, " 'Lazarus, come forth' " *(John 11:43, NASB)*. But when I opened my eyes I could not see, and when I tried to sit up, I could hardly move. As His words echoed around me, I struggled with my bonds until I finally sat, then stood. But my feet were so tightly wrapped that I could not walk, but merely hop toward what seemed to be light. I felt hands grabbing me and holding me steady, while other hands tore away the covers from my eyes. I found no words as my eyes beheld a multitude gathered behind Jesus. " 'Unbind him, and let him go' " *(John 11:44, NASB)* Jesus commanded, and it was then I knew that I had been dead. Dead! . . . I was dead, and Jesus made me live. When I remember Jesus, I remember death, and new life.

JAMES: *(Nodding in agreement)* Is that not what we all have known—death and new life. Yes, my brothers and sisters, we each have passed from death to life because of Him. Let us always remember this. Perhaps that is what He meant when He said, "In remembrance of Me." Here, take this cup and share it among you. For Jesus said " 'This cup is the new covenant in my blood. Do this . . . in remembrance of me' " *(1 Cor. 11:25, RSV)*. So do we remember the Lord Jesus.

ALL: In remembrance of the Lord Jesus.

NARRATOR: As the cup was shared from person to person, each one drank and remembered Jesus, and each story was different, and each story was the same.

The Stinging Death
by Louis May III

(Easter)

Characters: 8 voices, both male and female

(In heart-beat rhythm, one or more clap heels of hands together. Start with slow and quiet beat. Over a period of 30 seconds increase intensity to a rapid, frenzied pulse. Insistent and LOUD. Then stop abruptly. Wait five beats.)

ALL: *(Solemn and strong)* DEATH! It has come. It has overcome!

VOICE 1: It is Dark.

VOICE 2: Dismal.

VOICE 3: Bitter.

VOICE 4: And *Terrifying.*

ALL: "For the wages of sin is *death!*" *(Rom. 6:23, NKJV)*

VOICES 5-8: Death!

VOICES 3, 4: Death!

VOICE 2: Death!

ALL: "For *all* have sinned, and come *short* of the glory of God" *(Rom. 3:23, KJV).*

VOICE 1: Death reigns. The tomb is full with evil doers from all nations.

ALL: EVIL DOERS! Evil doers everywhere!

(In the following ten lines, each shouts out line, then repeats the line hissingly till all have shouted their line. Build intensity.)

VOICE 1: Slanderers.

VOICE 2: Boasters.

VOICE 3: Haters of God.

VOICE 4: Murderers.

VOICE 5: Coveters.

VOICE 6: Inventors of evil.

VOICE 7: Arrogant ones.

VOICE 8: Faithless ones.

VOICE 1: Cruel and treacherous ones.

VOICE 2: And gossippers.

(Voice 2 holds out this last shout, fading it out slowly. Others copy this fade with the hissing of their lines.)

ALL: They were *fully* aware of God's righteous decree that those who do such things *deserve* to *die.*

MALE: "Hear now this, O foolish people" *(Jer. 5:21, KJV).*

ALL: " 'Do you not fear me?' " says the Lord" *(Jer. 5:22, NKJV).*

VOICE 5: " 'Will you not tremble at my presence?' " *(Jer. 5:22, NKJV)*

ALL: "You are a rebellious people. You do not say in your heart, " 'Let us now fear the Lord' " *(Jer. 5:23-24, NASB, paraphrased).*

VOICE 6: "Who gives the refreshing rain in its season" *(Jer. 5:24, NASB paraphrased).*

VOICE 7: And who appoints the time for the harvest so that we may taste fresh vegetables and fine bread.

ALL: "Your sins have turned these things away. Your sins have withheld many good things from you" *(Jer. 5:25, NKJV paraphrased).*

VOICE 8: "There are wicked men among you" *(Jer. 5:26, NASB paraphrased).*

ALL: "They lie in wait to trap you in their schemes. Their houses are full of deceit" *(Jer. 5:26-27, NASB para-*

phrased).

(Wait a beat.)

ALL: "The Lord says, 'Shall I not punish them for these things? Shall I not avenge myself on such a people?' " *(Jer. 5:29, NKJV paraphrased)*

VOICE 3: *(Sternly)* Yes. The Lord will avenge Himself. He has already avenged Himself.

(Wait three beats.)

VOICES 4-6: *(Loud shriek)* "My God, my God, why have You forsaken me?" *(Ps. 22:1a, NKJV)*

VOICES 7, 8: "Why are You so far from helping me?" *(Ps. 22:1b, NKJV)*

VOICE 1: *(Pleadingly)* "You don't even hear the words of my groaning" *(Ps. 22:1c, NKJV paraphrased).*

VOICE 2: "I cry out in the day and in the night, but you do not hear me" *(Ps. 22:2, NASB paraphrased).*

VOICE 3: "I am a worm. A reproach of men, and despised of the people" *(Ps. 22:6, NKJV paraphrased).*

VOICES 4, 5: "All those who see me laugh me to scorn; they shake their head at me and say . . ." *(Ps. 22:7, NKJV paraphrased)*

ALL: *(Sarcastically)* "He trusted in the Lord, let the Lord rescue him. Let the Lord deliver him since he delights in the Lord" *(Ps. 22:8, NKJV paraphrased).*

VOICES 6-8: The Lord has avenged Himself. He has already delivered the sting of death.

VOICE 1: And on one not worthy of that sting.

(Wait two beats.)

ALL: What shall *we* do?

VOICE 2: For death came by man and we shall all die as the first man.

ALL: We came from the dust. We shall return to the dust!

VOICES 3-5: To decay and rot.

VOICES 6-8: For there is *no hope.* There is no hope.

ALL: "For the living know that they will die; but the dead know nothing" *(Eccl. 9:5a, NKJV).*

VOICES 1-4: "The dead have no reward. Even the memory of them is forgotten" *(Eccl. 9:5b, NKJV paraphrased).*

VOICES 5-8: "And look at the oppressed and their tears! They have no comforter. No comforter at all" *(Eccl. 4:1, NKJV paraphrased).*

ALL: "Cursed be the day in which I was born! Let the day not be blessed in which my mother bore me! Why did I come forth from the womb to see labor and sorrow, that my days should be consumed with shame?" *(Jer. 20:14,18, NKJV)*

VOICES 1-2: "Why is my pain perpetual?" *(Jer. 15:18, NKJV)*

VOICES 3-4: "My wound[s] incurable?" *(Jer. 15:18, NKJV)*

VOICES 5-6: My sorrow unending?

VOICES 7-8: My heart laboring?

ALL: "Your iniquities separate you from God; and your sins hide His face from you. He will not hear you" *(Isa. 59:2, NIV paraphrased).*

VOICES 3-6: "Your hands are defiled with blood, and your fingers with iniquity" *(Isa. 59:3a, NKJV).*

VOICES 1-2: "Your lips have spoken lies, and your tongue speaks perversities" *(Isa. 59:3b, NKJV paraphrased).*

VOICES 7-8: "Your paths are crooked . . . and so, you shall not know peace" *(Isa. 59:8, NKJV paraphrased).*

ALL: You will not know peace, but death will reign over you and corruption will destroy you.

VOICES 1-6: Destroy.

VOICES 7-8: Destroy.

ALL: "The last . . . to be destroyed is death" *(1 Cor. 15:26, NIV).*

VOICES 1-2: "For God has put all things under His feet" *(1 Cor. 15:27, NKJV paraphrased).*

(Wait a beat.)

VOICES 5-6: "So let us search out and examine our ways, and turn back to God" *(Lam. 3:40, NKJV paraphrased).*

VOICES 3-4: "Let us lift our hearts and hands to God in heaven. We have transgressed and rebelled" *(Lam. 3:41-42a, NKJV).*

VOICES 7-8: "You have not pardoned. You have covered Yourself with anger and pursued us; You have slain us without pity" *(Lam. 3:42b-43, NKJV paraphrased).*

ALL: "You have covered Yourself with a cloud, that prayer cannot pass through. I called on Your name, O Lord, from the lowest pit" *(Lam. 3:44,55, NKJV paraphrased).*

VOICE 1: "You have heard my voice" *(Lam. 3:56a, NKJV).*

VOICES 2-3: "Do not hide Your ear from my sighing," *(Lam. 3:56b, NKJV)*

VOICES 4-8: "From my cry for help" *(Lam. 3:56c, NKJV).*

ALL: "You drew near to me on the day I called to You, and said . . . " *(Lam. 3:57, NKJV paraphrased)*

VOICE 8: *(Whisper)* "Do not fear!" *(Lam. 3:57, NKJV)*

VOICES 5-7: *(Whisper)* "Do not fear."

VOICES 1-4: "Do not fear."

ALL: "God said, Do Not Fear."

The Birth and Crucifixion of Christ
by Matthew Trent Tullos

(Christmas, Easter)

Characters: 2 voices

This reading works well with script in hand. Singing "Sweet Little Jesus Boy" and "Were You There," after this reading provides a nice bridge into the next act of worship.

#1: "So it was, that, while they were there, the days were accomplished that she should be delivered" *(Luke 2:6, KJV).*

#2: "And Pilate answered them, 'What should I do unto him you call "King of the Jews"?' "And they cried out, 'Crucify Him!' " *(Mark 15:12-13, KJV paraphrased)*

#1: "And she brought forth her first born son, and wrapped him in swaddling clothes, and laid him in a manger; because there was no room for them in the inn" *(Luke 2:7, KJV).*

#2: "And they clothed him with purple and fashioned a crown of thorns and put it about his head" *(Mark 15:17, KJV paraphrased).*

#1: "And there were in the same country shepherds abiding in the field, keeping watch over their flock by night" *(Luke 2:8, KJV).*

#2: "And they smote him on the head with a reed, and did spit upon him, and bowing their knees worshipped him" *(Mark 15:19, KJV).*

#1: "And the angel said unto them, Fear not: for, behold, I bring you good tidings of great joy, which shall be to all people" *(Luke 2:10, KJV)*.

#2: "And Jesus said unto him, Verily I say unto thee, Today shalt thou be with me in paradise" *(Luke 23:43, KJV)*.

#1: "For unto you is born this day in the city of David a Savior which is Christ the Lord" *(Luke 2:11, KJV)*.

#2: "Likewise also the chief priests mocking said among themselves with the scribes, . . . Let Christ the King of Israel descend now from the cross, that we may see and believe" *(Mark 15:31-32, KJV)*. "When Jesus therefore had received the vinegar, he said, It is finished: and he bowed his head, and gave up the ghost" *(John 19:30, KJV)*.

#1: "And suddenly there was with the angel a multitude of the heavenly host praising God, and saying, Glory to God in the highest . . . peace" *(Luke 2:13-14, KJV)*.

Sermon on the Mount
by Steve Phillips

(Bible study, church service)
(Based on Matt. 5:3-14,20,41;
6:9-13,33.)
Characters: Four or more voices

VOICE 1: "Blessed ..."
VOICE 2: "Blessed ..."
VOICE 3: "Blessed are the poor in spirit ..."
VOICES 2, 4: "For theirs ..."
VOICES 1, 3: "Is the kingdom ..." *(Pause)*
ALL: "Of heaven."
VOICES 1, 2, 4: "Blessed are they that mourn ..."
VOICE 3: "For they shall be ..."

VOICE 1: "Comforted."
VOICE 2: *(Quietly)* "Blessed."
VOICE 4: What?
VOICE 2: *(Louder)* "Blessed are the meek ..."
VOICE 3: "For they shall ..."
VOICES 1, 3: "Inherit the ..."
VOICES 1, 3, 4: "Earth."
ALL: "Blessed are they which do ..."
VOICES 2, 3, 4: "Hunger and thirst ..."
VOICES 3, 4: "After righteousness ..."
VOICE 4: "For they shall be ..."
ALL: "Filled."
VOICE 1: "Blessed are the merciful ..."
VOICE 3: "For they shall obtain mercy."
VOICE 2: "Blessed are the ..."
ALL: "Pure ..."
VOICE 4: "In heart ..."
VOICE 2: "For ..."
VOICES 3, 2: "They ..."
VOICES 2, 3, 4: "Shall ..."
ALL: "See God."
VOICES 1, 3: "Blessed are the peacemakers ..."
VOICES 2, 4: "For they shall be called ..."
VOICE 3: "The children of God."
VOICE 2: "Blessed are they ..."
VOICE 1: "Which are persecuted ..."
VOICE 4: "For righteousness' sake ..."
VOICE 3: "For theirs is the kingdom ..." *(Pause)*
ALL: "Of heaven."
VOICES 1, 2: "Blessed are you ..."
VOICE 1: "When men shall revile you ..."
VOICES 2, 3: "And persecute you ..."
VOICES 2, 3, 4: "And shall say all manner of evil against you falsely ..."
VOICE 1: "For my sake."

VOICE 4: Therefore ...

VOICES 1, 2, 3: "Rejoice!"

VOICE 3: "For . . . your reward is . . . in heaven." *(Luke 6:23, KJV)*

VOICE 2: So remember . . .

VOICE 4: "You are the salt of the earth."

VOICES 2, 3: And don't forget that . . .

VOICE 1: "You are the light of the world."

VOICE 2: "A city that is set on a hill cannot be hid." *(Matt. 5:3-10, KJV; vv. 11-14, RSV)*

VOICE 4: So . . .

VOICES 3, 1: "Except your righteousness"

VOICE 4: "Exceed the"

VOICES 2, 4: "Righteousness of the Pharisees,"

VOICE 1: "You shall in no case"

VOICES 1, 2: "Enter into the kingdom" *(Pause)*

ALL: "Of heaven" *(Matt. 5:20, KJV)*.

VOICE 3: "And if someone asks you to go a mile,"

VOICE 2: "Go with him two" *(Matt. 5:41, RSV)*.

VOICE 4: And when you pray,

VOICE 1: Pray after this manner:

(Each of the four Voices *says their part simultaneously with the other three. They should all try to time it so they end at the same time.)*

VOICE 1: "Our Father which art in heaven, Hallowed be thy name."

VOICE 2: "Thy kingdom come. Thy will be done in earth, as it is in heaven."

VOICE 3: "Give us this day our daily bread. And forgive us our debts, as we forgive our debtors."

VOICE 4: "And lead us not into tempta-tion, but deliver us from evil."

ALL: "For thine is the kingdom,"

VOICES 1, 2, 3: "And the power,"

VOICES 1, 2: "And the glory,"

VOICE 1: "For ever."

ALL: "Amen." *(Matt. 6:9-13, KJV)*

VOICE 1: *(After a pause)* And one more thing, if you'll seek first the kingdom of God,

VOICE 2: And his righteousness,

VOICE 3: Then all your needs

VOICE 1: Like:

(Said very quickly)

VOICE 2: Eating,

VOICE 3: Drinking,

VOICE 4: Sleeping,

VOICE 2: What to wear,

VOICE 3: Where to work,

VOICE 4: And how to pay the bills. *(Pause)*

VOICE 3: Yes, all these things

ALL: Shall be added unto you. *(Matt. 6:33, paraphrased) (Repeat three times, getting softer each time. On the last line, pause before the last word, "you.")*

Recreation
by Lawanda Smith

Characters: 3 speakers

#1: I was created . . .

#2: To walk with Him.

#3: But I stumbled by myself.

#2: To share His love.

#3: But I hoarded my loneliness.

#2: To show His peace.

#3: But I created strife.

#2: To live His joy.

#3: But I died in unhappiness.

#2: To touch His people.

#3: But I withdrew into myself.

#2: To care for His earth.

#3: But I destroyed my abode.

#2: To make the most of His time.

#3: But I wasted what I called my own.

#2: To praise His name.

#3: But I kept silent.

#2: To shine His light.

#3: But I smothered any ember.

#1: In His image?

#2: And yet He was killed—He died . . .

#3: Willingly!

#2: For me!

#3: When I was not even the shadow of His likeness.

#1: And I am recreated.

#2: Now!

All: In His image.

#1: "Therefore if any man be in Christ, he is a new creature: old things are passed away; behold, all things are become new" *(2 Cor. 5:17, KJV)*.

Lord's Supper Worship Emphasis
by R. Wayne Johnson

(Based on John 3:16; 8:12; Isa. 9:6; John 6:50; Matt. 26:28; Pss. 139:23,.51:10.)

Characters: 3 voices

#1: God so loved ... !

#2: God so loved the world ... !

#3: God so loved the world that He gave
...

#2: He gave His only Son ...

#3: For us ...

#1: For you and for me.

#3: God so loved the world that He gave ...

#2: God took the initiative in Bethlehem when He became a human being in the person of Jesus Christ. He joined us

in the darkness of life and said, "I am the light of the world" *(John 8:12, KJV)*.

#1: The dark forest of human existence was made light.

(Pause)

#1: He walked among us here ...

#3: He experienced our needs ...

#2: He looked beyond hunger ...

#3: *(Quickly)* ... "things" ...

#1: *(Quickly)* ... the immediate ...

#3: He saw that He was our greatest need *then* and for eternity.

(Pause)

#2: "For unto us a child is born, unto us a son is given."

#1: His name is Wonderful, Counselor
...

#3: Mighty God, Everlasting Father ...

#2: The Son of man—Savior, Shepherd, Sacrifice.

#1: The Lamb of God.

(Pause)

#2: God so loved the world that He gave His Son ...

#3: To die!

#1: For us!

#2: For you and for me.

#3: To meet our greatest need.

(Pause)

#1: And the witness is this, that God has given us eternal life and this life is in His Son.

#2: "Here is the bread that comes down from heaven, which a man may eat and not die" *(John 6:50, NIV)*.

#1: And, "this is my blood of the covenant, which is poured out for many for the forgiveness of sins" *(Matt. 26:28, NIV)*.

#2: For us.

#3: For you and me.

(Pause)

#1: "Search me, O God, and know my heart. . . . See if there is any offensive way in me" *(Ps. 139:23, NIV)*.

#2: "Create in me a clean heart, O God" *(Ps. 51:10, KJV)*.

#3: Give me a generous heart, an obedient spirit.

#1: He asks our heart, our heads . . .

#2: . . . our abilities, our days . . .

#1: . . . our possessions, our willingness . . .

#3: God so loved the world that He gave . . .

#2: For you and for me.

#1: For our every need.

#3: For eternity and for now!

#2: We celebrate His sacrifice here tonight.

#1: And we examine our sacrifice for Him.

#3: For and through Jesus Christ our Lord.

Amen!

FUN DRAMA FOR FELLOWSHIPS

An Island Myth
by Juanita Hammond

Cast: King Kaahaamaahaau, Queen Namahanaau, Princess Lalialanakamilaau, King Nahaloco, Hollywood Agent
Setting: At the grass hut of the King and Queen.

KING: Today's the day.
QUEEN: Alas, alas.
KING: Perhaps he has forgotten.
QUEEN: Oh, I wish.
KING: Perhaps he is sick.
QUEEN: You are just wishing.
KING: Perhaps he has found another.
QUEEN: There is no one as beautiful as our Lalialanakamilaau.
KING: Lalialanakamilaau—beautiful princess.
PRINCESS: *(Enters)* Did I hear my name?
QUEEN: Ohhh . . . boo hoo . . .
PRINCESS: Father King, why is my Mother Dear crying?
KING: She always cries at weddings.
PRINCESS: Wedding? Oh, I *love* weddings. Who is getting married?
QUEEN: Ohhh . . . boo hoo . . .
KING: You are my dear.
PRINCESS: Me? Oh, but never. I have vowed never to marry. You said I could only marry King Nahaloco. And I don't want to marry him. He has a wart on his nose . . . and very big ears! He's ugly! And, you would have ugly grandchildren!
QUEEN: Ohhh . . . boo hoo . . .
KING: Oh, Lalialanakamilaau . . . I wish it were not so. But I promised. King Naholoco's father saved my life.
PRINCESS: Saved your life?
KING: Yes, I was trapped in the jungle by ferocious animals in the bush. There could have been a hundred . . . such crashing of bushes you never heard . . . and there was no path of escape.
QUEEN: It turned out to be just a land turtle . . . but he already promised.
PRINCESS: What did you promise?
KING: That I would give my daughter to marry his son on her 19th birthday.
PRINCESS: Today is my birthday.
QUEEN: Or more your death.
PRINCESS: I *would* rather die! Can you not pay him money?
KING: I thought of that but we have no money. There are no more pineapples, no more coconuts. Our grass hut is not even our own.
PRINCESS: Maybe we could strike oil?
QUEEN: Here?
KING: Oh, I am so foolish.
(King Nahaloco enters.)
LOCO: I have come for my bride.
PRINCESS: I refuse.

94

LOCO: You cannot refuse. Your father promised. My bride . . . or his head!

QUEEN: (Cries)

PRINCESS: (Cries)

AGENT: (Enters and bows before the King and Queen). Good day my dear friends. I am from Paradise Studios in Hollywood, California, and I was told I would find a great new star on this island.

PRINCESS: Oh father, may I go?

KING: A Hollywood star . . . much money!

QUEEN: We would be world famous!

KING: You could pay the debt and we could move back into the palace.

QUEEN: We could have luaus again!

KING: We would have money!

QUEEN: We would get on "20/20" . . . and Johnny Carson's show!

PRINCESS: (Primping) A movie queen!

AGENT: I think you misunderstood! I am not thinking of your daughter.

QUEEN: But no one is as beautiful as our Lalialanakamilaau!

AGENT: Lalialanakamilaau! (Looks at Princess.) Oh, to be sure.

KING: Then it is settled. May we have an advance? About $5,000 would be good. There is no time to delay.

AGENT: But—I don't want your daughter!

KING, QUEEN & PRINCESS: You don't?!

AGENT: No. I want this man. (Takes arm of King Nahaloco.) We are filming a sensational monster movie and we need a very ugly face. Very ugly!

KING: Very ugly!

PRINCESS & QUEEN: Very ugly!

(Agent and King Nahaloco exit.)

KING: There goes our money!

QUEEN: There goes "The Tonight Show"!

PRINCESS: At least I don't have to marry King Nahaloco!

LOCO: (Enters and takes arm of Princess.) I almost left without you. (They exit.)

KING: There goes our beautiful Princess Lalialanakamilaau!

QUEEN: Maybe we could still be on television!

KING: How do you imagine that to be possible?

QUEEN: On "Ripley's Believe It or Not"! We will certainly be the grandparents of the ugliest grandchildren in the world!

(King and Queen exit.)

Hit and Run Comedy
Compiled by Don Blackley

(Fellowships, parties)

Characters: 2 males, 2 females

Actors could dash up from the audience for each of the three sequences and immediately turn their backs to the audience or they could be in place with backs to the audience as a curtain is drawn. The characters in each joke rotate to face the audience as they say their lines, then turn their backs upon completion of the joke. Timing and good reading of the lines is all important.

Sequence 1

(1)

MALE #1: He stole my car!—He stole my car!

MALE #2: Take it easy now—Did you get a good look at him?

95

MALE #1: No, but I got his license number.

(2)

FEMALE #3: Do you know what it means when you see three elephants walking down the street in purple sweaters?

FEMALE #4: They're all on the same team.

(3)

MALE #1: Did you hear about the woman heart surgeon who was a failure? She had always heard the way to a man's heart was through the stomach.

(4)

MALE #2 to #1: (*Irate father to son*): "I sacrificed everything I had to send you to medical school (*Pause*) and now you tell me I have to quit smoking."

(5)

FEMALE #3: There once was a lady from Guam
Who said, "Now the ocean's so calm
I will swim for a lark."
She encountered a shark.
Let us now sing the 90th Psalm.

(6)

MALE #1: Say, what's the idea of wearing my raincoat?

MALE #2: Well, you wouldn't want your new suit to get wet would you?

Sequence II

(1)

FEMALE #4: With a car like that my advice is to keep it moving.

MALE #2: Why?

FEMALE #4: If you ever stop, the cops might think it's an accident.

(2)

FEMALE #3: They shot my dog Fido today.

MALE #1: Was he mad?

FEMALE #3: Well, he sure wasn't very pleased about it.

(3)

FEMALE #4: My boyfriend is so dumb that he thinks Shirley Temple is a synagogue.

(4)

MALE #1: Judge, I wantum changeum my name.

MALE #2: What is your name?

MALE #1: Chief Screeching Train Whistle.

MALE #2: What do you want to change it to?

MALE #1: Toots (*Snicker*)

(5)

FEMALE #4: Professor, do you think I'll ever be able to do anything with my voice?

MALE #2: Well, it might come in handy in case of fire or shipwreck.

(6)

MALE #1: Hi, how much milk will you need this week?

FEMALE #3: Thirty-nine quarts.

MALE #1: Thirty-nine quarts!? Why so much?

FEMALE #3: Why, I take my beauty baths in it.

MALE #1: Do you want it pasteurized?

FEMALE #3: No, just about right up to here.

Sequence III

(1)

FEMALE #4: I knew something was going to happen to our sweet little daughter in college.

MALE #1: What in the world has happened?

FEMALE #4: She is going to marry a

Chinaman.

MALE #1: How do you know?

FEMALE #4: (*Holding up imaginary letter*) Listen, I'll read it to you. Dear Mamma, I have fallen in love with Ping-Pong.

(2)

MALE #2: Let's see Pastor, the bill on the repairs on your car comes to a pretty sizeable figure.

MALE #1: Remember, I'm a poor preacher.

MALE #2: Yes, I know that, (*Pause*), I've heard you several times.

(3)

FEMALE #3: I'm afraid my husband doesn't love me anymore.

FEMALE #4: You mustn't jump to conclusions.

FEMALE #3: But I can't help being uneasy.

FEMALE #4: Why do you think your husband doesn't love you anymore?

FEMALE #3: He's been gone five years and I haven't heard a word from him.

(4)

FEMALE #4: Do you know why my hand is like a pie?

MALE #2: No, why?

FEMALE #4: Cause it's got my rang (*ring*) on it.

(5)

FEMALE #3: I'm forgetting men!

FEMALE #4: Me too . . . I'm forgetting a couple of them as soon as possible!

(6)

MALE #1: I want to try on that suit in the window.

MALE #2: I'm sorry sir, you'll have to use the dressing room.

Romance Without Words
by Debbie Howell

Props needed: Whip, bell, play money, pitcher, broom, mop, paintbrush, fishing line, socks, sand pail, banana, "Night" and "Curtain" signs

We are pleased to bring you a play without words—really it is a play upon words.

It is the exciting story of Henritta Von Asterbilt and her own true love—Harold the Hero.

Anyway we will narrate this tragic tale of love because even though they are beautiful and handsome—they are not very bright. You might even say they are downright dumb.

Don't be surprised at anything they do—because we have told them to do exactly as we say and to follow the story word for word. As our scene opens, Vernon the Villain is pouring over his bills. (*Raises pitcher and pours.*) Vernon is having money problems so he tries to whip his bills into shape. (*Whips the money.*)

He is broke, he wrings his hands, as he can see no way out. (*Rings bell above each hand.*)

Suddenly a thought strikes him. (*Spins as if struck in the face.*)

Vernon has the answer to his problems, he will marry the wealthy Henritta and all his money problems will be over.

But alas another thought strikes him. (*Spins again.*)

Henritta does not love him and she will never marry him—what can he do? Vernon is in such a mess. (*Vernon mouths words and pantomimes actions.*)

"I know what I'll do, I'll kidnap her and hold her hostage until she agrees to marry me."

Now we take you to the home of the fair Henritta.

Her maid Amanda creeps into the room quietly. (*Creeps in on all fours.*)

She is waiting for her mistress to return from a shopping spree—suddenly the door opens, and Henritta sweeps into room. (*Sweeping with broom.*)

Henritta is expecting a visit from Harold the Hero.

She is happy as she trips around the room. (*Walks in large circle, tripping as she goes.*)

Henritta is not happy for long. Vernon the villain enters.

Amanda sees him first and tries to give him the brush off. (*With paintbrush*)

Vernon convinces Amanda he means no harm, in fact he hands her quite a line. (*Fishing line*)

So Amanda decides to leave.

Henritta sees Vernon coming toward her, she screams and turns a little pale. (*Rotates sand pail on floor.*)

"A-ha my proud beauty," says Vernon. "You won't escape me now. I will take you to my dungeon until you agree to marry me."

Henritta pleads and tries to appeal to him. (*Hands him banana.*)

"Your appeal is fruitless"—laughs Vernon.

Henritta cries out—"Will no one save me?"

Suddenly Harold rushes in—(*Nothing happens.*) I said Harold rushes in (*Harold rushes in, then exits.*) and stays in (*Harold returns with mop.*)

He advances on Vernon—you scoundrel.

Harold threatens to mop the floor with Vernon.

Now the fight gets rough and Vernon socks Harold. (*With gym sock*)

Suddenly Harold finishes the fight with a surprise punch. (*Can of punch from floor*)

Vernon knows he is defeated and leaves with despair. (*Other sock from pocket, holding them up as he exits.*)

Harold invites Henritta to fly away with him. (*Flaps arms*)

As night falls and so does our curtain. (*Actors carrying signs saying NIGHT and CURTAIN enter and fall. All return and bow.*)